D0271423

HEINEMANN

SHAKESPEARE

Macbeth

edited by Frank Green

with additional notes and activities by
Rick Lee and Victor Juszkiewicz

Series Editor: John Seely

*In association with the RSA
Shakespeare in Schools Project*

The RSA Shakespeare in Schools Project

The **Heinemann Shakespeare Series** has been developed in association with the **RSA Shakespeare in Schools Project**. Schools in the project have trialled teaching approaches to make Shakespeare accessible to students of all ages and ability levels.

John Seely has worked with schools in the project to develop the unique way of teaching Shakespeare to 11- to 16-year-olds found in **Heinemann Shakespeares**.

The project is a partnership between the RSA (Royal Society for the encouragement of Arts, Manufacture and Commerce), Leicestershire County Council and the Groby family of schools in Leicestershire. It is co-ordinated by the Knighton Fields Advisory Centre for Drama and Dance.

Heinemann Educational Publishers
Halley Court, Jordan Hill, Oxford OX2 8EJ
a division of Reed Educational & Professional Publishing Ltd
OXFORD   MELBOURNE   AUCKLAND
JOHANNESBURG   BLANTYRE   GABORONE
IBADAN   PORTSMOUTH (NH) USA   CHICAGO

Introduction, notes and activities © Frank Green, John Seely, Rick Lee 1994
Additional material by Victor Juszkiewicz

The text is based on J. Dover Wilson's Facsimile Edition of the First Folio 1623, but modern scholars have been freely consulted and used.

Published in the *Heinemann Shakespeare Plays* series 1994

05 04 03 02 01 00 99 98
18 17 16 15 14 13 12

A catalogue record for this book is available from the British Library on request.
ISBN 0 435 19203 5

Cover design Miller Craig and Cocking
Cover photograph from Donald Cooper

Produced by Green Door Design Ltd

Printed by Clays Ltd, St Ives plc

CONTENTS

Introduction: using this book

This is more than just an edition of *Macbeth* with a few notes.
It is a complete guide to studying and enjoying the play.

It begins with an introduction to Shakespeare's theatre,
and to the story and characters of the play.

At the end of the book there is guidance on studying the
play:
- how to keep track of things as you work
- how to take part in a range of drama activities
- understanding Shakespeare's language
- exploring the main themes of the play
- studying the characters
- how to write about the play.

There are also questions and a glossary of specialist words
you need when working on the play.

The central part of the book is, of course, the play itself.
Here there are several different kinds of help on offer:

Summary: at the top of each double page there is a short
summary of what happens on that page.

Grading: alongside the text is a shaded band to help you
when working on the play:

1 This is very important text that you probably need to
spend extra time on.

2 This is text that you need to read carefully.

3 This is text that you need to spend less time on.

Notes: difficult words, phrases and sentences are explained
in simple English

Extra summaries: for the 'white' text the notes are
replaced by numbered summaries that give more detail than
the ordinary page-by-page summaries.

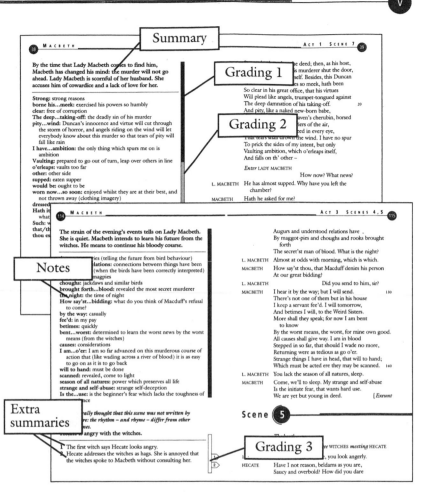

Activities

After every few scenes there is a section containing things to do, helping you to focus on the scenes you have just read:
- questions to make sure you have understood the story
- discussion points about the themes and characters of the play
- drama activities
- character work
- close study to help you understand the language of the play
- writing activities.

Shakespeare's theatre

Heavens the roof above the stage, supported by pillars. Characters could be lowered to the stage during the play

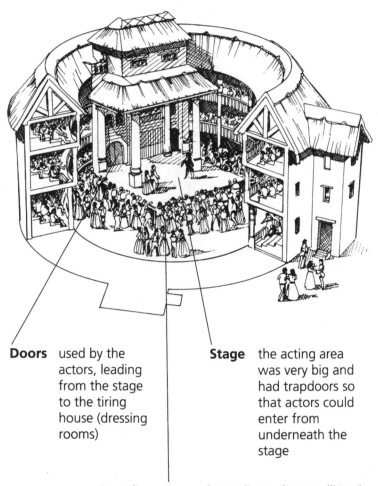

Doors used by the actors, leading from the stage to the tiring house (dressing rooms)

Stage the acting area was very big and had trapdoors so that actors could enter from underneath the stage

Standing space for audience ('groundlings')

Below is a scene from *Macbeth* showing both the inner stage
and the gallery in use for the action of the play.

When you have studied the play, you should be able to work
out exactly which moment in the play this shows.

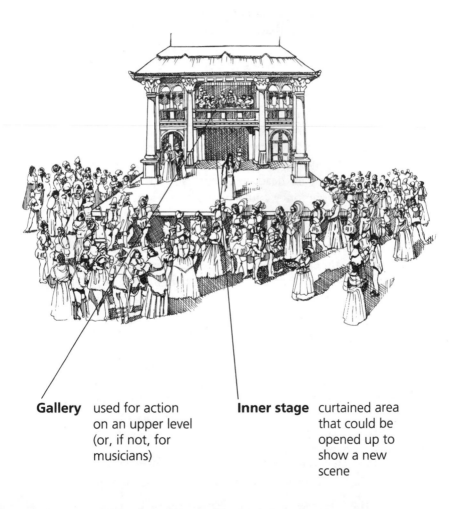

Gallery used for action
on an upper level
(or, if not, for
musicians)

Inner stage curtained area
that could be
opened up to
show a new
scene

Going to the theatre in Shakespeare's day

Theatre-going was very popular in Elizabethan London, but it was very different from going to a play today. It was like a cross between going to a football match and going to the theatre. The playhouses were open air and the lack of artificial lighting meant that plays were performed in daylight, normally in the afternoon.

Places were not reserved, so people had to arrive in plenty of time – often more than an hour before the play was due to start. They paid a penny to get into the playhouse, so it was not cheap, since a penny was about one twelfth of a day's wages for a skilled workman. Your penny let you into the large open yard surrounding the stage. The audience here had to stand, looking up at the actors (the stage was 1.5–1.8 metres above the ground). If people wanted a seat, then they had to pay another penny or twopence. This gave admission to the tiers of seating surrounding the yard, and also meant that you had a roof over your head, in case it started to rain. People with even more money could pay to have a seat in an enclosed room. So people of all incomes and social classes attended the theatre and chose the accommodation they wanted.

While the audience was waiting for the play to begin, people had time to meet friends, talk, eat and drink – in fact they used to continue to enjoy themselves in this way while the play was being performed. But Elizabethan audiences were knowledgeable and enthusiastic. Watching a play was an exciting experience; although the stage was very big, the theatre was quite small, so no-one was far from the actors. When an actor had a soliloquy (solo speech) he could come right into the middle of the audience and speak his thoughts in a natural, personal way. At the other extreme the large stage and the three different levels meant that whole battles could be enacted, complete with cannon fire, thunder and lightning and loud military music.

There was no painted stage scenery, so that the audience had to use their imagination to picture the location of each scene, but Shakespeare always gave plenty of word clues in the characters' speeches of when and where a scene took place. The lack of scenery to move about also meant that scene could follow scene without any break. On the other hand, the theatre companies spared no expense on costumes and furniture and other properties; plays also had live music performed by players placed either in the auditorium close to the stage, or in the gallery above it, if that was not to be used in the play.

Altogether Londoners especially must have considered that going to the theatre was an exciting and important part of their lives; it is believed that up to a fifth of them went to the theatre regularly. Shakespeare and the company in which he became a shareholder, the Lord Chamberlain's Men, worked hard and became wealthy men.

The characters of the play

Duncan

Malcolm

Donalbain

Macduff

Lennox

Banquo

Lady
Macduff

Fleance

Lady
Macduff's
Son

Ross

Captain

Witches

Two Murderers

Lady Macbeth

Macbeth

Seyton

Gentlewoman

Scottish Doctor

Porter

The story of the play

Macbeth and **Banquo**, co-leaders of the Scottish army, are returning from battle when they meet **three witches**. The witches prophesy that Macbeth will become Thane of Cawdor and, later, king. They tell Banquo that he will not be king himself but he will an ancestor of kings. Messengers arrive with the news that Macbeth has been made Thane of Cawdor. Macbeth begins to consider the possibility of becoming king! There is a chance that **King Duncan** might choose Macbeth, a cousin, as his successor, but Macbeth's hopes are dashed when Duncan names his son, **Malcolm**. Macbeth sees Malcolm as an obstacle to be overcome.

Lady Macbeth has received a letter from Macbeth, telling her of the prophecies and his new title. She is determined to help him become king, and when Macbeth returns, preceding Duncan who is to stay with them overnight, she persuades him to kill the king. When the body is discovered Duncan's sons fear for their own lives and flee. Macbeth is made king.

Remembering the witches' prophecy to Banquo, Macbeth hires murderers to kill Banquo and his son, **Fleance**. Fleance escapes, and Banquo's ghost returns to haunt Macbeth. He returns to the witches to try to find some consolation. Macbeth is told to be wary of **Macduff**, Thane of Fife; he is assured that he cannot be harmed by one 'born of woman', and that he will never be defeated until Birnam Wood moves to Dunsinane. Finally, Macbeth is shown a line of kings in the likeness of Banquo.

Macduff has not cooperated with Macbeth, and he goes to see Malcolm in England. Macbeth orders the deaths of Macduff's wife and family. Malcolm and Macduff lead an English army, reinforced by Scots sympathizers, against Macbeth. Lady Macbeth has gone mad and she dies. Approaching Macbeth's castle at Dunsinane, Malcolm's army cuts branches from the trees of Birnam Wood as camouflage. Macbeth's forces are easily defeated. Macbeth himself is killed by Macduff, who '*was from his mother's womb untimely ripp'd*'. Malcolm is made King of Scotland.

Background to the play

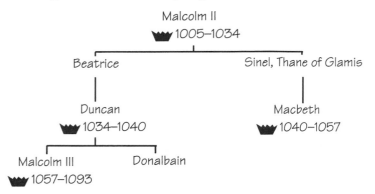

Malcolm II
1005–1034

Beatrice

Sinel, Thane of Glamis

Duncan
1034–1040

Macbeth
1040–1057

Malcolm III
1057–1093

Donalbain

The source of Macbeth

Shakespeare often found the ideas for his plays in historical sources. The lives of great rulers with their dramatic conflicts provided excellent plots for plays. Shakespeare did not follow his sources closely, however. Instead, he took all the most interesting parts and sometimes added new material to make his plays exciting on the stage.

Shakespeare used Holinshed's *Chronicles* as his source for *Macbeth*. In turn, Holinshed had based his work on earlier sources. The story of the life of Macbeth was first documented by John of Fordun, the father of Scottish history, in the fourteenth century. Later, in the sixteenth century, three other historians recorded the story: Hector Boece (or Boyce), George Buchanan and John Leslie. It was on these writings, and particularly those of Boece, that Raphael Holinshed based his account of this period of Scottish history in his *Chronicles of England, Scotland and Ireland* in 1577.

Shakespeare has made a number of alterations and additions to Holinshed. One major change is that the play covers a period of a few months, whereas Macbeth ruled Scotland for 17 years; another is that in reality Macbeth was a good king and Duncan was weak, but in the play Macbeth is a tyrant and Duncan is highly respected.

Some other changes are that in Holinshed:

- Lady Macbeth is mentioned only once
- the rebellion and invasion take place at different times
- Macdonwald commits suicide
- Duncan is killed by hired assassins
- the drugging of guards and their murder is from a different period of Scottish history
- Banquo is party to the death of Duncan
- Banquo is murdered after Macbeth's banquet, not before
- Macbeth flees from Macduff.

Note: the witches are in Holinshed, but *not* the apparitions, Banquo's ghost and the show of kings.

Jacobean background

In 1603 Shakespeare's company of actors came under the patronage of James I, and they were known as the King's Men. Macbeth was probably first performed at court in August 1606 to mark the visit of James's brother-in-law, King Christian of Denmark.

Out of respect for his royal audience, Shakespeare made certain omissions from the historical story:

- Banquo knows nothing of the plot to kill Duncan
- Mary Queen of Scots is missing from the 'show of kings'
- no mention is made of the Danes who reinforced Sweno's army.

On the other hand, it is not surprising that on such an occasion Shakespeare included elements of which James I would approve:

- the qualities of good kingship (James had written a treatise on the art of government)
- the divine nature of kings
- the healing powers of kings
- James's family tree, including Banquo and Edward the Confessor
- the condemnation of the equivocation of Garnet (see page 64)
- the supernatural.

Witchcraft

During the reign of Queen Elizabeth I (1533–1603) the public were increasingly preoccupied with witchcraft. In 1564 a law came into force making murder by witchcraft punishable by death, thus acknowledging witches and their supernatural powers. It is estimated that in Scotland alone 8,000 witches were burned to death between 1564 and 1603.

In 1604 an additional law was passed in Scotland, which declared that anyone found guilty of practising witchcraft should be executed. James I himself became personally involved with witchcraft when he and his wife, Anne, were almost shipwrecked on their return to Scotland from Denmark in 1590. In a notable case, a Dr Fian and the 'witches of Berwick' were found guilty of trying to kill them by raising storms at sea.

James I published a work on witchcraft, *Demonology*, in 1597. Although some people rebelled against this persecution, the belief in witches was widespread and the execution of witches did not cease until the end of the seventeenth century.

Divine order

Jacobeans believed that the whole universe had an order to it which was decided by God. Anything unnatural was against this divine order. Kings were God's agents, so action against a king was a crime against God. Satan had rebelled against God directly, and he was responsible, through witches and evil spirits, for all attacks on the divine order.

About the play

Although it is set in Scotland in 1040, *Macbeth* deals with issues which are relevant to any society in any age. It explores the far-reaching effects of one man's ambition, from the total transformation of that man's character to the nation-wide terror which he provokes.

At the beginning of the play Macbeth is co-leader of the Scottish army and a national hero. He increases his reputation with further victories, but a prophecy that he is to become king changes his life, and the lives of his fellow Scots, as he embarks on a course of evil.

The means by which this transformation is achieved would have fascinated Shakespeare's contemporary audience, who were intrigued by – and fearful of – the supernatural. Today's audience takes less literally the witches, the apparitions, the ghost and the '*air-drawn*' dagger, but we appreciate the notion of the supernatural and the reality of the driving force of ambition.

Once Macbeth's course of action is established (committing a series of evil acts because his ambition has been stirred by the supernatural) Shakespeare hints to the audience what Macbeth's fate will be; who will be responsible for making sure that he pays for his crimes. Most of the scenes in the last two acts of the play are concerned with structuring the action to bring Macbeth, eventually, face-to-face with the means by which justice is finally done.

MACBETH

CHARACTERS

DUNCAN, King of Scotland
MALCOLM, his son
DONALBAIN, his younger son
BANQUO, a Thane (nobleman of Scotland)
FLEANCE, Banquo's son
MACDUFF, Thane of Fife
LADY MACDUFF, his wife
SON OF MACDUFF
MACBETH, Thane of Glamis, later Thane of Cawdor and King of
   Scotland
LADY MACBETH, his wife
GENTLEWOMAN, her attendant
SEYTON, Macbeth's armour bearer
PORTER at Macbeth's castle
CAPTAIN wounded in battle
AN OLD MAN
DOCTOR of physic
1ST MURDERER
2ND MURDERER
3RD MURDERER
ROSS ⎫
LENNOX ⎪
MENTEITH ⎬   other thanes
ANGUS ⎪
CAITHNESS ⎭
Three WITCHES, the weird sisters
HECATE, Queen of Witchcraft

Three APPARITIONS
Three OTHER WITCHES
SIWARD, Earl of Northumberland
YOUNG SIWARD, his son
ENGLISH DOCTOR at the court of King Edward the Confessor

Lords, Soldiers, Attendants, Servants and Messengers

SCENE *Scotland and England*

Three witches immediately establish the influence of the supernatural. They are to meet Macbeth when a battle is over.

Thunder and lightning: in superstitious times it was believed
    that fierce storms released forces of evil, and were omens of
    unrest in individual people and whole countries
hurlyburly: fighting
ere: before
Greymalkin: the name of a grey cat. Each witch had a
    familiar, a link with the spirit world. (The familiars are
    calling the witches.)
Paddock: a toad, another familiar
Anon: at once
Fair is foul...fair: to the witches, what is evil is good: what is
    good they find repulsive. (This is their attitude to life, but it
    could also be a warning to the audience that things to follow
    are not what they might seem.)
Hover: (not a 'natural' movement)
fog and filthy air: (Is this an 'atmosphere' associated with the
    witches? It certainly has no connection with thunder and
    lightning.)

Duncan, King of Scotland, meets a wounded captain.

plight: condition

Act one

Scene 1

An open place

Thunder and lightning. Enter three WITCHES

1ST WITCH	When shall we three meet again
	In thunder, lightning, or in rain?
2ND WITCH	When the hurlyburly's done,
	When the battle's lost and won.
3RD WITCH	That will be ere the set of sun.
1ST WITCH	Where the place?
2ND WITCH	Upon the heath.
3RD WITCH	There to meet with Macbeth.
1ST WITCH	I come Greymalkin!
2ND WITCH	Paddock calls.
3RD WITCH	Anon! 10
ALL	Fair is foul, and foul is fair;
	Hover through the fog and filthy air.

[Exeunt

Scene 2

A camp near the battlefield

Alarum within. Enter DUNCAN, MALCOLM,
DONALBAIN, LENNOX, *with* ATTENDANTS, *meeting a
bleeding* CAPTAIN

DUNCAN	What bloody man is that? He can report,
	As seemeth by his plight, of the revolt

The wounded captain reports that Macbeth has defeated the rebellion of Highlanders and Islanders, led by Macdonwald. No sooner was that battle over than Sweno, King of Norway, began an attack on the tired Scottish army.

---

sergeant: (referred to as *captain* elsewhere)
broil: battle
spent: exhausted
choke their art: prevent each other from swimming
to that: to that end; to make him a rebel
villainies: evil qualities
Western Isles: Hebrides
kerns and gallowglasses: infantry and cavalry
fortune: Fortune, a notoriously unreliable goddess
quarrel: cause
whore: mistress
all: (i.e. Macdonwald and the extra forces and Fortune)
Disdaining: disregarding
brandished steel: drawn sword
smoked with bloody execution: steamed with blood
valour's minion: bravery's favourite
slave: (a contemptuous reference to Macdonwald)
Which: who (Macbeth)
unseamed him...chops: split him open from the navel to the
    jaw
cousin: Duncan and Macbeth were grandsons of King
    Malcolm, whom Duncan succeeded
whence: from where (refers to the East)
reflection: shining
So from that...Discomfort swells: at the moment of triumph
    further danger arises (the calm before the storm)
justice: (the Scottish army had right on their side)
skipping: quick-footed (in running away!)
Norweyan lord: Sweno, King of Norway
surveying vantage: seeing his chance
furbished: well-polished; i.e. well-prepared

The newest state.

MALCOLM   This is the sergeant
Who like a good and hardy soldier fought
'Gainst my captivity. Hail brave friend.
Say to the King the knowledge of the broil
As thou didst leave it.

CAPTAIN   Doubtful it stood,
As two spent swimmers, that do cling together
And choke their art. The merciless Macdonwald –
Worthy to be a rebel, for to that   10
The multiplying villainies of nature
Do swarm upon him – from the Western Isles
Of kerns and gallowglasses is supplied,
And fortune on his damned quarrel smiling
Showed like a rebel's whore. But all's too weak,
For brave Macbeth – well he deserves that name –
Disdaining fortune, with his brandished steel,
Which smoked with bloody execution,
Like valour's minion carved out his passage,
Till he faced the slave;   20
Which ne'er shook hands, nor bade farewell to
    him,
Till he unseamed him from the nave to the chops,
And fixed his head upon our battlements.

DUNCAN   O valiant cousin, worthy gentleman!

CAPTAIN   As whence the sun 'gins his reflection
Shipwrecking storms and direful thunders break,
So from that spring, whence comfort seemed to
    come,
Discomfort swells. Mark King of Scotland, mark.
No sooner justice had, with valour armed,
Compelled these skipping kerns to trust their
    heels,   30
But the Norweyan lord, surveying vantage,
With furbished arms, and new supplies of men,
Began a fresh assault.

Macbeth and Banquo led their men with renewed vigour. At this point the captain collapses from his wounds and is taken for treatment. Ross completes the tale of the victory against the Norwegians.

As sparrows (dismay) **eagles, or the hare** (dismays) **the lion:** (irony)
sooth: truly, truth
cracks: charges of gunpowder
Except: unless
reeking: steaming
memorize: make memorable, famous
Golgotha: 'the place of the skull' where Jesus was crucified
Thane: a Scottish title, roughly equivalent to an earl
seems to: is about to
flout: mock
fan our people cold: (with fear)
Bellona's bridegroom: Mars, the Roman god of war, was husband to Bellona
lapped in proof: clad in armour
Confronted...self-comparisons: matched him in every way
curbing: restraining
lavish: insolent

DUNCAN   Dismayed not this
Our captains, Macbeth and Banquo?

CAPTAIN   Yes,
As sparrows eagles, or the hare the lion.
If I say sooth, I must report they were
As cannons overcharged with double cracks, so
    they
Doubly redoubled strokes upon the foe.
Except they meant to bathe in reeking wounds,
Or memorize another Golgotha,   40
I cannot tell –
But I am faint, my gashes cry for help.

DUNCAN   So well thy words become thee as thy wounds,
They smack of honour both. Go get him
    surgeons.

                                    [*Exit* CAPTAIN, *attended*

Enter ROSS *and* ANGUS

Who comes here?

MALCOLM   The worthy Thane of Ross.

LENNOX   What a haste looks through his eyes! So should he
    look
That seems to speak things strange.

ROSS   God save the King!

DUNCAN   Whence camest thou, worthy Thane?

ROSS   From Fife, great King,
Where the Norweyan banners flout the sky,
And fan our people cold. Norway himself,   50
With terrible numbers,
Assisted by that most disloyal traitor,
The Thane of Cawdor, began a dismal conflict,
Till that Bellona's bridegroom, lapped in proof,
Confronted him with self-comparisons,
Point against point, rebellious arm 'gainst arm,
Curbing his lavish spirit; and to conclude,

Duncan pronounces the death sentence on the treacherous Thane of Cawdor, and says that Macbeth shall now have that title.

craves composition: begs for peace terms
deign: allow
disbursed: paid up
Saint Colme's Inch: Inchcolm, an island in the Firth of Forth
dollars: (sixteenth-century coins, not eleventh-century)
bosom: dearest, closest
present: immediate
lost/won: (contrast – see also Act 1 scene 1 line 11,
    '*foul/fair*', and Act 1 scene 2 lines 27–28,
    '*comfort/discomfort*')

Whilst awaiting the arrival of Macbeth, the witches discuss their spiteful treatment of a sea-captain.

Killing swine: (witches were often held responsible for the
    death of animals)
Aroint thee: Get lost!
rump-fed ronyon: fat-bottomed hag (Note: The woman
    responds to the witch in this fearless way, presumably,
    because her religious belief makes her immune from evil.
    The witch decides to take out her spite on the woman's
    husband.)
sieve: (the traditional vessel of witches)
a rat without a tail: (when witches transformed themselves
    into animals they were usually incomplete)
I'll do: I'll take revenge

The victory fell on us.

DUNCAN   Great happiness!

ROSS   That now
Sweno, the Norways' King, craves composition.
Nor would we deign him burial of his men   60
Till he disbursed, at Saint Colme's Inch,
Ten thousand dollars to our general use.

DUNCAN   No more that Thane of Cawdor shall deceive
Our bosom interest. Go pronounce his present
      death,
And with his former title greet Macbeth.

ROSS   I'll see it done.

DUNCAN   What he hath lost noble Macbeth hath won.

                                          [*Exeunt*

Scene 3

A heath

Thunder. Enter three WITCHES

1ST WITCH   Where hast thou been, sister?

2ND WITCH   Killing swine.

3RD WITCH   Sister, where thou?

1ST WITCH   A sailor's wife had chestnuts in her lap,
And munched, and munched, and munched – 'Give
      me,' quoth I.
'Aroint thee witch,' the rump-fed ronyon cries.
Her husband's to Aleppo gone, master o' th'
      Tiger,
But in a sieve I'll thither sail,
And like a rat without a tail,
I'll do, I'll do, and I'll do.   10

2ND WITCH   I'll give thee a wind.

The witches continue their story. Macbeth and Banquo enter on their way to report to Duncan at Forres.

I myself...shipman's card: I control the other winds and know which ports they blow on from every point of the compass.

dry as hay: (he will not be able to put in to port for water)

Sleep: (sleep – or lack of it – is a recurring theme in the play)

penthouse lid: eyelid like a sloping roof

forbid: accursed

peak: waste away

pilot's thumb: (parts of corpses were used in casting spells)

Posters: speedy travellers

Thrice: (The number three, and multiples of three, were regarded as magic numbers – see line 22. Note also the repetition of words or phrases, as '*I'll do*' in line 10.)

So foul and fair a day: (Macbeth probably refers to the weather and the victories) Note echo of scene 1 line 11.

attire: clothing

aught: anything

aught...question: (Banquo fears they are evil spirits)

1ST WITCH	Th' art kind.
3RD WITCH	And I another.
1ST WITCH	I myself have all the other,
	And the very ports they blow,
	All the quarters that they know
	I' the shipman's card.
	I'll drain him dry as hay;
	Sleep shall neither night nor day
	Hang upon his penthouse lid.
	He shall live a man forbid;
	Weary sev'n-nights nine times nine
	Shall he dwindle, peak, and pine.
	Though his bark cannot be lost,
	Yet it shall be tempest-tossed.
	Look what I have.
2ND WITCH	Show me, show me.
1ST WITCH	Here I have a pilot's thumb,
	Wrecked as homeward he did come.

20

[Drum within

3RD WITCH	A drum, a drum!
	Macbeth doth come.
ALL	The Weird Sisters, hand in hand,
	Posters of the sea and land,
	Thus do go about, about,
	Thrice to thine, and thrice to mine,
	And thrice again, to make up nine.
	Peace, the charm's wound up.

30

Enter MACBETH *and* BANQUO

MACBETH	So foul and fair a day I have not seen.
BANQUO	How far is't called to Forres? What are these,
	So withered, and so wild in their attire,
	That look not like th' inhabitants o' th' earth,
	And yet are on't? Live you, or are you aught
	That man may question? You seem to understand
	me,

40

Each witch greets Macbeth differently: Thane of Glamis,
Thane of Cawdor and '*that shalt be King hereafter*'. Banquo
asks what the witches have to say to him. They tell
Banquo that his descendants will be kings. Macbeth tries
to question the witches.

choppy: chapped
hereafter: in the future
why do you start?: (Have the witches struck a chord in
   Macbeth? Do they know his inner thoughts?)
fantastical: imaginary
present grace...royal hope: (reference to the predictions)
rapt withal: carried away with it (also a play on words, *wrapt
   with all:* involved with everything)
look into...which will not: see how things are going to
   develop
get: beget, be the ancestor of
imperfect: leaving things unspoken
Sinel: Macbeth's father
prosperous: thriving, healthy
prospect of belief: realms of possibility
owe: get
intelligence: information

By each at once her choppy finger laying
Upon her skinny lips. You should be women,
And yet your beards forbid me to interpret
That you are so.

MACBETH   Speak if you can. What are you?

1ST WITCH   All hail Macbeth, hail to thee, Thane of Glamis!

2ND WITCH   All hail Macbeth, hail to thee, Thane of Cawdor!

3RD WITCH   All hail Macbeth, that shalt be King hereafter!   50

BANQUO   Good sir, why do you start, and seem to fear
Things that do sound so fair? I' th' name of truth
Are ye fantastical, or that indeed
Which outwardly ye show? My noble partner
You greet with present grace, and great prediction
Of noble having, and of royal hope,
That he seems rapt withal. To me you speak not.
If you can look into the seeds of time,
And say which grain will grow, and which will not,
Speak then to me, who neither beg nor fear   60
Your favours nor your hate.

1ST WITCH   Hail!

2ND WITCH   Hail!

3RD WITCH   Hail!

1ST WITCH   Lesser than Macbeth, and greater.

2ND WITCH   Not so happy, yet much happier.

3RD WITCH   Thou shalt get kings, though thou be none.
So all hail Macbeth and Banquo!

1ST WITCH   Banquo and Macbeth, all hail!

MACBETH   Stay you imperfect speakers, tell me more.   70
By Sinel's death I know I am Thane of Glamis,
But how of Cawdor? The Thane of Cawdor lives
A prosperous gentleman; and to be king
Stands not within the prospect of belief,
No more than to be Cawdor. Say from whence
You owe this strange intelligence, or why

The witches disappear. Macbeth and Banquo begin to discuss what has happened. Ross and Angus enter and Macbeth learns that he is the Thane of Cawdor.

---

blasted: blighted
charge: command
The earth...are of them: they disappear like air-bubbles
corporal: to be flesh
Would: I wish
insane root: root of a plant which causes hallucinations
Thane of Cawdor: (the audience is reminded of this prediction immediately before the entrance of Ross)
personal venture: own feats of bravery
His wonders...thine or his: he struggles to express praise for your deeds because he is so amazed by them
Silenced with that: this conflict in his mind has made him speechless
Strange images of death: unnatural forms of death
post: messenger
herald: accompany
earnest: pledge
greater honour: (Does this remind Macbeth of the third prediction, and raise his hopes?)

Upon this blasted heath you stop our way
With such prophetic greeting? Speak, I charge you.

[WITCHES *vanish*

BANQUO The earth hath bubbles, as the water has,
And these are of them. Whither are they
          vanished?   80

MACBETH Into the air; and what seem'd corporal melted
As breath into the wind. Would they had stayed.

BANQUO Were such things here as we do speak about?
Or have we eaten on the insane root
That takes the reason prisoner?

MACBETH Your children shall be kings.

BANQUO   You shall be King.

MACBETH And Thane of Cawdor too; went it not so?

BANQUO To th' selfsame tune and words. Who's here?

Enter ROSS *and* ANGUS

ROSS The King hath happily received, Macbeth,
The news of thy success; and when he reads   90
Thy personal venture in the rebels' fight,
His wonders and his praises do contend,
Which should be thine or his. Silenced with that,
In viewing o'er the rest o' th' selfsame day,
He finds thee in the stout Norweyan ranks,
Nothing afeard of what thyself didst make,
Strange images of death. As thick as hail
Came post with post, and every one did bear
Thy praises in his kingdom's great defence,
And poured them down before him.

ANGUS   We are sent   100
To give thee from our royal master thanks,
Only to herald thee into his sight,
Not pay thee.

ROSS And for an earnest of a greater honour,
He bade me, from him, call thee Thane of Cawdor;

Banquo and Macbeth are shocked. Banquo warns
Macbeth that evil is at work, and that, despite appearing
favourable at the moment, there is something sinister in
the predictions. Macbeth begins to consider what it will
mean if the third prediction is to come true.

---

addition: title
dress...robes: (The imagery of clothing recurs throughout the
   play. We have already seen '*unseamed*', scene 2 line 22, and
   are about to see '*line*', scene 3 line 112.)
heavy judgement: sentence of death
was combined: joined forces
line: give support
vantage: benefit
wrack: ruin
capital: deserving the death penalty
behind: still to come
trusted home: believed absolutely
enkindle you unto: make you desire
But 'tis strange: It is unnatural/supernatural (Banquo gives
   Macbeth a serious warning, which is ignored – until Act 5
   scene 8!)
And oftentimes...consequence: The forces of evil encourage
   us to bring about our own destruction, by giving us accurate
   information about things which are trivial, and misleading us
   on important matters.
Cousins: friends
a word, I pray you: (Banquo takes Ross and Angus on one
   side)
truths: (repeating Banquo's '*truths*', line 124)
happy prologues...imperial theme: promising forerunners to
   the increasing splendour of the royal story (Macbeth sees
   himself as the central character in a play.)
I thank you, gentlemen: (Is Macbeth thanking Ross and
   Angus again; or asking them to move further away to give
   him time to think?)
soliciting: prompting
ill/good: (contrast again)
earnest: promise

In which addition, hail most worthy Thane,
For it is thine.

BANQUO [*Aside*]   What, can the devil speak true?

MACBETH The Thane of Cawdor lives. Why do you dress me
In borrowed robes?

ANGUS   Who was the Thane lives yet,
But under heavy judgement bears that life 110
Which he deserves to lose. Whether he was
 combined
With those of Norway, or did line the rebel
With hidden help and vantage, or that with both
He laboured in his country's wrack, I know not;
But treasons capital, confessed and proved,
Have overthrown him.

MACBETH [*Aside*]   Glamis, and Thane of Cawdor.
The greatest is behind. [*To* ROSS *and* ANGUS]
 Thanks for your pains.
[*To* BANQUO] Do you not hope your children shall
 be kings,
When those that gave the Thane of Cawdor to me
Promised no less to them?

BANQUO   That, trusted home, 120
Might yet enkindle you unto the crown,
Besides the Thane of Cawdor. But 'tis strange:
And oftentimes, to win us to our harm,
The instruments of darkness tell us truths,
Win us with honest trifles, to betray's
In deepest consequence.
Cousins, a word I pray you.

MACBETH [*Aside*]   Two truths are told
As happy prologues to the swelling act
Of the imperial theme. – I thank you gentlemen. –
[*Aside*] This supernatural soliciting 130
Cannot be ill, cannot be good.
If ill, why hath it given me earnest of success,
Commencing in a truth? I am Thane of Cawdor.

Macbeth decides to let the future take care of itself, and he and Banquo agree to discuss matters at a more convenient time.

---

yield: give in

suggestion: temptation

horrid image: (Macbeth pictures himself as Duncan's murderer)

doth unfix my hair: makes my hair stand on end

Against the use of nature: unnaturally

Present fears: real causes of fear

My thought...surmise: murder is only a thought going through my mind, and yet I am so shaken by it that I am unable to act

nothing is But what is not: what I imagine is the only thing that exists for me

rapt: absorbed

Without my stir: without my having to do anything

strange garments...aid of use: new clothes do not fit properly until they have worn for a time (imagery of clothing again)

Come what...roughest day: whatever happens, stormy days come to an end (The rhyming couplet indicates an end to his thoughts on this matter.)

we stay upon your leisure: we are waiting until it suits you

favour: pardon

wrought: troubled

things forgotten: things I was trying to remember

where every day...read them: in my memory

chanced: happened

The interim having weighed it: having considered this matter in the meantime

Our free hearts: openly

If good, why do I yield to that suggestion,
Whose horrid image doth unfix my hair,
And make my seated heart knock at my ribs,
Against the use of nature? Present fears
Are less than horrible imaginings.
My thought, whose murder yet is but fantastical,
Shakes so my single state of man, that function   140
Is smothered in surmise, and nothing is
But what is not.

BANQUO   Look how our partner's rapt.

MACBETH   [*Aside*] If chance will have me King, why chance
                may crown me
            Without my stir.

BANQUO   New honours come upon him,
            Like our strange garments, cleave not to their
                mould
            But with the aid of use.

MACBETH   [*Aside*]   Come what come may,
            Time and the hour runs through the roughest day.

BANQUO   Worthy Macbeth, we stay upon your leisure.

MACBETH   Give me your favour: my dull brain was wrought
            With things forgotten. Kind gentlemen, your
                pains   150
            Are registered where every day I turn
            The leaf to read them. Let us toward the King.
            [*To* BANQUO] Think upon what hath chanced, and
                at more time,
            The interim having weighed it, let us speak
            Our free hearts each to other.

BANQUO   Very gladly.

MACBETH   Till then enough. – Come friends.

                                        [*Exeunt*

ACTIVITIES

Keeping track

Scene 1

1 Who do the witches intend to meet, when and where?

Scene 2

2 Which enemies have Macbeth and Banquo defeated?
3 How is Macbeth to be rewarded?

Scene 3

4 Which prophecy comes true for Macbeth almost immediately?
5 Which prophecy to Macbeth still has to be fulfilled?
6 What was the prophecy concerning Banquo?

Discussion

1 Two armies have been prepared to try to overthrow Duncan. From this, what can we assume about conditions in Scotland, and possibly about Duncan's capabilities as king?
2 In scene 3 lines 39–88, is Banquo's attitude to the witches any different from Macbeth's? Does one of them take the witches more seriously than the other, for instance? From these lines find one quotation for Banquo and one for Macbeth which sums up each character's feelings about the witches at this stage.

Drama

1 Divide the witches' lines between the whole class. This could be done in a variety of ways: small groups of twos and threes have a line or sentence each; or some people speak the lines whilst others provide the thunder and lightning background. Practise these lines – you will find them very easy to learn.(Why do you think that is?) Experiment with the volume, ranging

from screaming to whispering. Experiment with the tone of your voices; perhaps harsh, sarcastic or sweetly nice.

Eventually you should fashion a soundscape that is frightening, even spine-chilling. You could then record it.

2 What do these witches look like? There are clues in this scene and others. (Illustrations elsewhere in this book are only one person's idea of what they might look like. We all have our own vision of them.)

Imagine that you have been commissioned as designers for a production of the play. The designer has not yet decided on an overall look or period. She wants you to interest her with ideas, the more unusual the better. Present your drawings to your teacher, who can take the role of director. Be prepared to justify your designs by referring to the text.

3 'Look how our partner's rapt' (scene 3 line 142)

In this scene Macbeth talks to himself a lot, whilst his companions stand close by. What are they thinking?
Use FORUM THEATRE (see page 228), to explore their relationships and how their feelings can be shown or hidden.

Either a volunteer or your teacher could take the role of Macbeth and say his lines, whilst the others become his companions.

Remember that Banquo is his friend, has just fought alongside him in two successful battles and has also heard the witches' prophecies. Ross and Angus may be unaware of the witches, but they may have some feelings about the news they have been sent to deliver to Macbeth – and about the way in which he receives the news.

Before this encounter they were all roughly equal. How are things changing?

Character

1 What sort of man is Duncan? What sort of king is he?
   - Remember that it was usual for an eleventh-century king to lead his army himself.
   - What do you think of his responses in scene 2 (especially lines 24, 33–34 and 58) and the fact that peace terms have been decided without consulting him (lines 63–65)?
2 Malcolm is to be quite an important figure in the play. What little do we learn about him from scene 2? Do you have any feelings about him at all? If so, are they favourable or not?
3 • What qualities of Macbeth are we told about in scene 2? Has he made a favourable impression before we even see him?
   - Do Macbeth's thoughts at the end of Scene 3 tell us more about him? Is he still making a favourable impression?
4 Begin CHARACTER LOGS (see page 212) on Macbeth, Duncan, Banquo and Malcolm.

Close study

1 The opening scene of most plays provides the audience with information and sets the tone of the rest of the play.
   - What information is provided in scene 1 of this play?
   - How is that information reinforced in lines 1–23 of scene 2?
   - How does scene 1 set the tone for the rest of this play?
2 Since Shakespeare first wrote this play, the soldier who reports to Duncan has been called both 'sergeant' and 'captain'.
   - Looking at the language of his report, can you suggest why modern editors prefer 'captain'?
   - Are there any particular phrases, or lines, or images in the captain's report which impress you? Why?
   - Is there anything about Ross's report (scene 2 lines 48–58) which shows that he was merely an observer of the battle, rather than a participant like the captain?
3 In your own words, what is Banquo's warning to Macbeth in scene 3 lines 122–126?

Writing

1 Using the information provided in scene 2, write a brief report
   on the battles for King Duncan. Your report will need to be
   factual (where the battles took place, who was involved, and so
   on) but at the end, under the heading 'Comments', you can
   add your own thoughts and observations.
2 Banquo and Macbeth are making their way back after the
   battles to report to Duncan. What are they talking about?
   Remember that they are co-leaders of Duncan's army, and
   probably have been friends for years. Their families might share
   many social occasions. They know each other extremely well.
   In script form, write the conversation between Banquo and
   Macbeth, ending with Macbeth's '*So foul and fair a day I have
   not seen.*'

Quiz

Who said the following, and to whom?
   1 '*So well thy words become thee as thy wounds*'
   2 '*that shalt be king hereafter*'
   3 '*Thou shalt get kings, though thou be none*'

Who said the following, and about whom?
   4 '*O valiant cousin, worthy gentleman!*'
   5 '*Go pronounce his present death*'
   6 '*What are these,
       So withered, and so wild in their attire*'

Who said the following, when, and about what?
   7 '*he unseamed him from the nave to th' chops*'
   8 '*Dismayed not this
       Our captains, Macbeth and Banquo?*'
   9 '*I'll drain him dry as hay*'
  10 '*Two truths are told
       As happy prologues to the swelling act*'

The Thane of Cawdor has been executed. Duncan thanks Macbeth profusely for his part in the victories. Macbeth modestly says that he was only doing his duty.

---

in commission: who were given the responsibility of making sure that the sentence was carried out

Became him like: was as worthy as

had been...death: had practised how to die

owed: owned

careless: worthless

trifle: thing of no importance

There's no art...face: there is no way to judge how a man thinks from how he looks

He was...absolute trust: (dramatic irony – enter Macbeth!)

Was: weighs

Thou art...overtake thee: Your value to me is so far ahead, that, however I try to repay you, I cannot catch up

swiftest wing: (bird imagery)

the proportion...mine: I might have been able to repay you in proportion to my gratitude

all: everything I have

Only I...all can pay:
    1 rhyming couplet to 'round off' this idea;
    2 Irony – *all* is exactly what Macbeth wants!

In doing...itself: are their own reward

Scene 4

Forres

Flourish. Enter DUNCAN, MALCOLM, DONALBAIN, LENNOX, *and* ATTENDANTS

DUNCAN   Is execution done on Cawdor? Are not
Those in commission yet returned?

MALCOLM   My liege,
They are not yet come back. But I have spoke
With one that saw him die; who did report
That very frankly he confessed his treasons,
Implored your Highness' pardon, and set forth
A deep repentance. Nothing in his life
Became him like the leaving it; he died
As one that had been studied in his death,
To throw away the dearest thing he owed,   10
As 'twere a careless trifle.

DUNCAN   There's no art
To find the mind's construction in the face.
He was a gentleman on whom I built
An absolute trust.

Enter MACBETH, BANQUO, ROSS *and* ANGUS

                     O worthiest cousin,
The sin of my ingratitude even now
Was heavy on me. Thou art so far before,
That swiftest wing of recompense is slow
To overtake thee. Would thou hadst less deserved,
That the proportion both of thanks and payment
Might have been mine. Only I have left to say,   20
More is thy due than more than all can pay.

MACBETH   The service and the loyalty I owe,
In doing it pays itself. Your Highness' part
Is to receive our duties; and our duties

Duncan names Malcolm as his successor, and then invites
himself to Macbeth's castle. Macbeth sees that 'chance'
will not make him king, and he makes up his mind to do
something about it.

Safe toward: to ensure (see lines 13–14!)
plant...growing: (horticultural imagery)
There if...your own: if I flourish, you will benefit
plenteous joys: so many reasons for happiness
Wanton in fulness: abundant to saturation point
harvest plenteous wanton fulness: (horticultural imagery)
We: (the royal plural)
establish our estate upon: name as successor to the throne
Prince of Cumberland: (customary title of the heir to the
    Scottish throne) Now that the kingdom has been made safe
    – by Macbeth! – Duncan chooses his successor. The oldest
    son did not automatically succeed in Scotland, and Duncan
    could have chosen from any of his close relations – including
    Macbeth (see note on scene 2 line 24)
But signs...deservers: honours will be distributed widely
Inverness: the site of Macbeth's castle
bind us further: make me more indebted
The rest...for you: it is only a chore when I am not serving
    you
harbinger: messenger
that is...o'erleap: Malcolm is an obstacle to the throne which
    I must overcome
Stars...desires: (blackness – of night and evil acts – is a
    recurring image of the play)
wink at: be blind to
be: be done
For in my way...to see: (two rhyming couplets at the end
    emphasize Macbeth's resolve to act)

Are to your throne and state, children and servants,
Which do but what they should be doing every
        thing
Safe toward your love and honour.

DUNCAN   Welcome hither.
I have begun to plant thee, and will labour
To make thee full of growing. Noble Banquo,
That hast no less deserved, nor must be known   30
No less to have done so. Let me infold thee,
And hold thee to my heart.

BANQUO   There if I grow,
The harvest is your own.

DUNCAN   My plenteous joys,
Wanton in fulness, seek to hide themselves
In drops of sorrow. Sons, kinsmen, Thanes,
And you whose places are the nearest, know,
We will establish our estate upon
Our eldest, Malcolm, whom we name hereafter
The Prince of Cumberland; which honour must
Not unaccompanied invest him only,   40
But signs of nobleness, like stars, shall shine
On all deservers. From hence to Inverness,
And bind us further to you.

MACBETH   The rest is labour, which is not used for you.
I'll be myself the harbinger, and make joyful
The hearing of my wife with your approach;
So humbly take my leave.

DUNCAN   My worthy Cawdor.

MACBETH   [*Aside*] The Prince of Cumberland – that is a step,
On which I must fall down, or else o'erleap,
For in my way it lies. Stars hide your fires,   50
Let not light see my black and deep desires.
The eye wink at the hand; yet let that be,
Which the eye fears when it is done to see.   [*Exit*

DUNCAN   True worthy Banquo; he is full so valiant,

commendations: praises
peerless: without equal

Lady Macbeth reads a letter from her husband, telling of the witches' predictions. She knows Macbeth has ambition, but fears he is too noble to make sure that the prediction is fulfilled.

perfect'st report: most reliable information
missives: messengers
deliver: tell
dues: due share
'They met…and farewell': (the letter is in prose to mark it off from the blank verse of speech)

milk of human kindness: inner goodness
catch the nearest way: take by the most direct method
wouldst: want to be
illness: evil
What thou…holily: you want greatness, but only by fair means
wouldst wrongly win: would take what you should not have
That which cries…have it: the crown which cries 'You must do this' if you want it

And in his commendations I am fed;
It is a banquet to me. Let's after him,
Whose care is gone before to bid us welcome.
It is a peerless kinsman.   [*Flourish. Exeunt*

Scene 5

Macbeth's castle

Enter LADY MACBETH, *reading a letter*

L. MACBETH   'They met me in the day of success; and I have
learned by the perfect'st report, they have more in
them than mortal knowledge. When I burned in
desire to question them further, they made
themselves air, into which they vanished. Whiles I
stood rapt in the wonder of it, came missives from
the King, who all-hailed me "Thane of Cawdor", by
which title, before these weird sisters saluted me,
and referred me to the coming on of time with
"Hail King that shalt be!" This have I thought   10
good to deliver thee, my dearest partner of
greatness, that thou mightst not lose the dues of
rejoicing by being ignorant of what greatness is
promised thee. Lay it to thy heart, and farewell.'
Glamis thou art, and Cawdor, and shalt be
What thou art promised; yet do I fear thy nature,
It is too full o' th' milk of human kindness
To catch the nearest way. Thou wouldst be great,
Art not without ambition, but without
The illness should attend it. What thou wouldst
                highly,   20
That wouldst thou holily; wouldst not play false,
And yet wouldst wrongly win. Thou'dst have,
                great Glamis,
That which cries 'Thus thou must do, if thou
                have it';

Lady Macbeth is startled to learn that Duncan is on his way to the castle. She calls on the evil spirits to make her ruthless so that she can carry out the murder of Duncan.

And that which: murder
Hie: hurry
chastise: whip
valour: boldness
impedes: prevents
golden round: crown
metaphysical: supernatural
tidings: news
Is not…preparation: (Lady Macbeth tries to cover up for her first startled response)
informed for preparation: let me know so that I could prepare
had the speed of: rode faster than
Give him tending: look after him
The raven…hoarse: the croaking raven, a bird of ill-omen, is more hoarse than usual because it signals Duncan's death (bird imagery)
my battlements: (Lady Macbeth sees herself solely responsible)
spirits…mortal thoughts: evil spirits that serve murderous thoughts
unsex me: take away my femininity
direst: most bitter
make thick…and it: prevent pity from flowing in my veins, make sure that I can feel no compassion so that no feelings of humanity upset my ruthless intention, nor stop me from carrying it out
take my milk for gall: replace my milk with bitterness
murd'ring ministers: spirits of murder
in your sightless substances: in your invisible state
wait on nature's mischief: look after humanity's evil deeds
thick night: (a plea for darkness; see scene 4 lines 50–51)
pall thee: cover yourself
dunnest: darkest

And that which rather thou dost fear to do
Than wishest should be undone. Hie thee hither,
That I may pour my spirits in thine ear,
And chastise with the valour of my tongue
All that impedes thee from the golden round,
Which fate and metaphysical aid doth seem
To have thee crowned withal.

Enter ATTENDANT

What is your tidings?   30

MESSENGER   The King comes here tonight.

L. MACBETH   Thou'rt mad to say it.
Is not thy master with him, who were't so
Would have informed for preparation.

MESSENGER   So please you, it is true; our Thane is coming.
One of my fellows had the speed of him
Who almost dead for breath, had scarcely more
Than would make up his message.

L. MACBETH   Give him tending,
He brings great news.   [*Exit* ATTENDANT
                   The raven himself is hoarse
That croaks the fatal entrance of Duncan
Under my battlements. Come you spirits   40
That tend on mortal thoughts, unsex me here,
And fill me from the crown to the toe top-full
Of direst cruelty; make thick my blood,
Stop up th'access and passage to remorse,
That no compunctious visitings of nature
Shake my fell purpose, nor keep peace between
Th' effect and it. Come to my woman's breasts,
And take my milk for gall, you murd'ring
   ministers,
Wherever in your sightless substances
You wait on nature's mischief. Come thick
   night,   50
And pall thee in the dunnest smoke of hell,

When Macbeth returns, Lady Macbeth urges him to hide his feelings and to leave everything to her.

my keen knife: (Does Lady Macbeth intend to commit the murder herself?)

Hold: stop

ignorant present: the present does not know what the future will be

Thy letters...purposes: (the murder of Duncan is hinted at)

O never...morrow see: (Lady Macbeth makes the intention clear)

  1 the sun will not shine for Duncan

  2 see Act 2 scene 4 lines 6–7

beguile the time: deceive the world

Look like the time: wear a suitable expression

flower/serpent: (biblical metaphor)

provided for/great business/dispatch: (play on words, all relating to murder)

Which shall...masterdom:

  1 tonight ensures our royal future

  2 this is the most important night of our lives

To alter...fear: an inappropriate expression always arouses suspicion

That my keen knife see not the wound it makes,
Nor heaven peep through the blanket of the dark,
To cry 'Hold, hold!'

Enter MACBETH

       Great Glamis, worthy Cawdor,
Greater than both, by the all-hail hereafter,
Thy letters have transported me beyond
This ignorant present, and I feel now
The future in the instant.

MACBETH   My dearest love.
Duncan comes here tonight.

L. MACBETH   And when goes hence?

MACBETH Tomorrow, as he purposes.

L. MACBETH   O never   60
Shall sun that morrow see.
Your face, my Thane, is a book where men
May read strange matters. To beguile the time,
Look like the time; bear welcome in your eye,
Your hand, your tongue; look like th' innocent
  flower,
But be the serpent under't. He that's coming
Must be provided for; and you shall put
This night's great business into my dispatch,
Which shall to all our nights and days to come
Give solely sovereign sway and masterdom.   70

MACBETH We will speak further.

L. MACBETH   Only look up clear;
To alter favour ever is to fear
Leave all the rest to me.   [*Exeunt*

The king and his retinue arrive at Inverness, and Duncan is greeted warmly by Lady Macbeth.

seat: situation
the air...senses: the fresh air is relaxing
temple-haunting martlet: house martin
mansionry: nest-building
jutty: part of a building which juts out
coign of vantage: suitable corner
pendent: hanging
procreant cradle: nest for its young
This castle...is delicate:
    1 the contrast between the mood of these lines and that of the previous scene is deliberate
    2 note the dramatic irony of Duncan's first lines – and his next lines!
The love...our trouble: the love of followers is sometimes inconvenient, but appreciated all the same. My coming here to show my love for you gives you the opportunity to ask God to reward me, and also to thank me personally, for having the chance to entertain me.
point: respect
single: feeble
house: family
those of old: former honours
late dignities heaped up to: recent honours on top of
hermits: people who pray for the souls of benefactors
coursed: chased

Scene 6

At the entrance of the castle

Oboes and torches. Enter DUNCAN, MALCOLM,
DONALBAIN, BANQUO, LENNOX, MACDUFF, ROSS,
ANGUS, *and* ATTENDANTS

DUNCAN   This castle hath a pleasant seat; the air
Nimbly and sweetly recommends itself
Unto our gentle senses.

BANQUO   This guest of summer,
The temple-haunting martlet, does approve,
By his loved mansionry, that the heavens' breath
Smells wooingly here. No jutty, frieze,
Buttress, nor coign of vantage, but this bird
Hath made his pendent bed and procreant cradle.
Where they most breed and haunt, I have
    observed
The air is delicate.

Enter LADY MACBETH

DUNCAN   See, see our honoured hostess. 10
The love that follows us sometime is our trouble,
Which still we thank as love. Herein I teach you,
How you shall bid God 'ild us for your pains,
And thank us for your trouble.

LADY MACBETH   All our service
In every point twice done, and then done double,
Were poor and single business to contend
Against those honours deep and broad wherewith
Your Majesty loads our house. For those of old,
And the late dignities heaped up to them,
We rest your hermits.

DUNCAN   Where's the Thane of Cawdor? 20
We coursed him at the heels, and had a purpose

Duncan is full of compliments for Macbeth and Lady Macbeth.

purveyor: official who went ahead to organize things for royal visits
holp: helped
Your servants...your own: your subjects are always ready to give you your due. (Your subjects always have their servants, themselves and everything they own ready to be accounted for, so that when the king wishes to check he can claim what is his.)

Outside the banqueting hall Macbeth thinks over the decision to murder Duncan.

If it...done quickly: if that were an end to it when the murder is committed, then it would be good to get it over with quickly
trammel: catch in a net
his surcease: Duncan's death
success: a good result/succession to the throne
here: in this world
bank/shoal: sandbank
jump: risk (also, clear/jump over)
the life to come: what happens in the life after death
these cases: murder
still: always
have judgement here: are sentenced on earth ('case'/ 'judgement')
that: in that
Bloody instructions: lessons in bloodshed
return...inventor: rebound on the person who started it
even-handed: well-balanced
Commends: recommends
ingredience: ingredients, contents
chalice: cup (of religious significance)
kinsman: relative

To be his purveyor; but he rides well,
And his great love, sharp as his spur, hath holp him
To his home before us. Fair and noble hostess,
We are your guest tonight.

L. MACBETH   Your servants ever
Have theirs, themselves, and what is theirs, in
            compt,
To make their audit at your Highness' pleasure,
Still to return your own.

DUNCAN   Give me your hand.
Conduct me to mine host, we love him highly,
And shall continue our graces towards him.   30
By your leave, hostess.   [*Exeunt*

Scene 7

A room in the castle

Oboes and torches. Enter a SEWER, *and divers*
SERVANTS *with dishes and service, and pass over the*
stage. Then enter MACBETH

MACBETH   If it were done, when 'tis done, then 'twere well
It were done quickly. If th' assassination
Could trammel up the consequence, and catch
With his surcease, success; that but this blow
Might be the be-all and the end-all – here,
But here, upon this bank and shoal of time,
We'd jump the life to come. But in these cases
We still have judgement here, that we but teach
Bloody instructions, which being taught return
To plague th' inventor. This even-handed justice   10
Commends th' ingredience of our poisoned
            chalice
To our own lips. He's here in double trust:
First, as I am his kinsman and his subject,

By the time that Lady Macbeth comes to find him, Macbeth has changed his mind: the murder will not go ahead. Lady Macbeth is scornful of her husband. She accuses him of cowardice and a lack of love for her.

Strong: strong reasons

borne his...meek: exercised his powers so humbly

clear: free of corruption

The deep...taking-off: the deadly sin of his murder

pity...wind: Duncan's innocence and virtue will cut through the storm of horror, and angels riding on the wind will let everybody know about this murder so that tears of pity will fall like rain

I have...ambition: the only thing which spurs me on is ambition

Vaulting: prepared to go out of turn, leap over others in line

o'erleaps: vaults too far

other: other side

supped: eaten supper

would be: ought to be

worn now...so soon: enjoyed whilst they are at their best, and not thrown away (clothing imagery)

dressed: (repeating Macbeth's metaphor)

Hath it...freely: has hope woken with a hangover, regretting what it said when it was drunk?

Such: worthless as a drunken promise

that/the ornament of life: both refer to the crown

thou esteem'st: you regard

Strong both against the deed; then, as his host,
Who should against his murderer shut the door,
Not bear the knife myself. Besides, this Duncan
Hath borne his faculties so meek, hath been
So clear in his great office, that his virtues
Will plead like angels, trumpet-tongued against
The deep damnation of his taking-off.   20
And pity, like a naked new-born babe,
Striding the blast, or heaven's cherubin, horsed
Upon the sightless couriers of the air,
Shall blow the horrid deed in every eye,
That tears shall drown the wind. I have no spur
To prick the sides of my intent, but only
Vaulting ambition, which o'erleaps itself,
And falls on th' other –

Enter LADY MACBETH

                       How now? What news?

L. MACBETH   He has almost supped. Why have you left the
               chamber?

MACBETH   Hath he asked for me?

L. MACBETH   Know you not he has?   30

MACBETH   We will proceed no further in this business.
               He hath honoured me of late, and I have bought
               Golden opinions from all sorts of people,
               Which would be worn now in their newest gloss,
               Not cast aside so soon.

L. MACBETH   Was the hope drunk
               Wherein you dressed yourself? Hath it slept since?
               And wakes it now to look so green and pale
               At what it did so freely? From this time
               Such I account thy love. Art thou afeard
               To be the same in thine own act and valour   40
               As thou art in desire? Wouldst thou have that
               Which thou esteem'st the ornament of life,
               And live a coward in thine own esteem,

When Macbeth begins to waver, Lady Macbeth explains her plan. Macbeth is impressed both by his wife's plan, and by her attitude.

Letting...'I would': letting fear get the better of desire

adage: proverb (the cat wanted fish, but would not wet her paws)

none: 1 there is no-one

2 not a man, but a superhuman

beast: (contrast with '*man*')

break this enterprise: suggest this plan

durst: dared to

to be more...were: to become king

Nor...nor: neither...nor

Did then adhere: were then convenient

would: were determined to

that their fitness...you: time and place are here and now, and you are unmanly/cowardly

I have given suck: I have had a child (Lady Macbeth was Macbeth's second wife, and she had a son to her first husband.)

I would...to this: (Lady Macbeth plays her womanliness against her husband's manliness)

If we should fail?: (Macbeth wavers)

But...sticking-place: only wind up your courage to its strongest point (like the tight string of a cross-bow)

chamberlains: attendants/guards

with wine...only: They will be so overcome by drink and making merry that memory, which is supposed to protect the brain, will melt in an alcoholic vapour; and the brain itself, receptacle ('*receipt*') of reason, will be like a vessel for for distilling alcohol. (i.e. They will be so drunk that they will remember nothing.)

drenched: drowned

What not...officers: we can blame the drunken guards for anything

quell: enterprise

undaunted mettle: determined spirit

Bring forth...males: (Macbeth is full of admiration for her planning and her confidence)

Letting 'I dare not' wait upon 'I would,'
Like the poor cat i' th' adage?

MACBETH   Prithee peace.
I dare do all that may become a man;
Who dares do more is none.

L. MACBETH   What beast was't then,
That made you break this enterprise to me?
When you durst do it, then you were a man;
And to be more than what you were, you would   50
Be so much more the man. Nor time nor place
Did then adhere, and yet you would make both.
They have made themselves, and that their fitness
      now
Does unmake you. I have given suck, and know
How tender 'tis to love the babe that milks me –
I would while it was smiling in my face
Have plucked my nipple from his boneless gums,
And dashed the brains out, had I so sworn as you
Have done to this.

MACBETH   If we should fail?

L. MACBETH   We fail?
But screw your courage to the sticking-place,   60
And we'll not fail. When Duncan is asleep –
Whereto the rather shall his day's hard journey
Soundly invite him – his two chamberlains
Will I with wine and wassail so convince,
That memory, the warder of the brain,
Shall be a fume, and the receipt of reason
A limbeck only; when in swinish sleep
Their drenched natures lie as in a death,
What cannot you and I perform upon
Th' unguarded Duncan? What not put upon   70
His spongy officers, who shall bear the guilt
Of our great quell?

MACBETH   Bring forth men-children only,
For thy undaunted mettle should compose

Macbeth is determined to carry out the murder.

received: accepted as true
other: otherwise
we shall...roar: we shall be loud in our sorrow and anger
bend up: (like a bow; see line 60)
Each corporal agent: every power in my body
mock the time: deceive the world
False face...doth know: (see scene 5 lines 63–66, 72)

CTIVITIES

Keeping track

Scene 4

1 What happened to the Thane of Cawdor? Why?
2 What is the connection between Duncan, Malcolm and the Prince of Cumberland?

Scene 5

3 Which word/s would you use to describe Lady Macbeth's reaction to Macbeth's letter: disappointed, pleased, excited, bored, determined, interested, uncontrolled?

Scene 6

4 What is the effect of lines 1–10, and especially line 1, after the events of Scene 5?

Scene 7

5 What has Macbeth decided by line 31?
6 What has Macbeth decided by the end of the scene?

Nothing but males. Will it not be received,
When we have marked with blood those sleepy two
Of his own chamber, and used their very daggers,
That they have done't?

L. MACBETH   Who dares receive it other,
As we shall make our griefs and clamour roar
Upon his death?

MACBETH   I am settled, and bend up
Each corporal agent to this terrible feat.   80
Away, and mock the time with fairest show:
False face must hide what the false heart doth know.
                                        [*Exeunt*

Discussion

1 Look at Macbeth's contribution to the dialogue in scene 5
   from his entrance at line 54 to the end of the scene. What do
   you think is going through his mind?
2 At the end of scene 5 Lady Macbeth says, '*To alter favour ever is
   to fear*'. It has been suggested that this means: if you change
   your mind, you had better watch out! Do you think that this
   is a good interpretation of the line?
3 '*What beast was't then, That made you break this enterprise to me?*'
   (scene 7 lines 47–48) Is this true? Was it Macbeth's idea? If
   not, why does Lady Macbeth say it was?
4 '*When you durst do it, then you were a man*' (scene 7 line 49)
   Macbeth rightly has a reputation as a man of action. His
   record as a soldier is unequalled. But is Lady Macbeth's
   suggestion a sign of manliness?
5 Is Lady Macbeth driven only by her wish to see Macbeth
   better himself, or does she have her own ambition – to
   become queen?

Drama

1   '*There's no art To find the mind's construction in the face*'
    (scene 4 lines 11–12). There are numerous times during
    these scenes when the irony of this line is emphasized.
    Look at:
    • the entrance of Macbeth (scene 4 line 14)
    • Duncan's embrace (scene 4 lines 28–29)
    • the announcement of the heir (scene 4 lines 37–38)
    • the entrance of the attendant (scene 5 line 30)
    • Macbeth's arrival home (scene 5 line 54)
    • the entrance of Lady Macbeth (scene 6 line 10).
    In small groups recreate these moments, concentrating on
    how Macbeth and Lady Macbeth disguise their real
    feelings. What does this do to their faces, hands and bodies?
    The soliloquies and asides the two characters make will
    provide you with a lot of ideas.
         Use FORUM THEATRE (see page 228) and FREEZE! (see
    page 227) to capture these moments. For example, when
    Duncan names Malcolm as his successor, Macbeth must
    look pleased; but inside he is thinking, '*Stars hide your fires...*'

2   Look at Lady Macbeth's speech, '*The raven himself is hoarse*'
    to '*cry "Hold, hold!"*'(scene 5 lines 38–54). Each person or
    small group in the class should learn a line or section.
    • Identify and emphasize those words and combinations of
      words that make alliterative or onomatopoeic sounds.
    • Divide the speech into syllables. See if you can find the
      pattern. Are there any irregularities? How could these
      help you say the words?
    • What actions is Lady Macbeth performing during this
      speech?
    • Experiment with the volume and tone.
    This is one of the most exciting and dramatic events in the
    play. See if you can feel and project some of its electric
    power.

3   Imagine you are a soldier on the battlements of Macbeth's
    castle. From your vantage point you are able to see the
    argument between Macbeth and Lady Macbeth (scene 7

lines 28–82) through a window, *but* you cannot hear it. What would it look like?

In groups of three use the script to decide what the movements would be to accompany these lines. Two of you represent the husband and wife; the third is the director/observer.

Follow up

When he comes off duty the soldier can re-tell what he saw to:
- his colleagues
- his sergeant, who has heard rumours of an argument
- Ross.

Character

1 Malcolm's report of the Thane of Cawdor's death (scene 4 lines 2–11) says a lot about that treacherous gentleman. But from what he says, and the way he says it, what do you learn about Malcolm? When Duncan names Malcolm as his successor do you think it is entirely inappropriate? Malcolm is young, but Duncan expects to live for some time and intends to groom his son to succeed him. Does Malcolm seem to have personal qualities which would make him a good king?

2 a The first time we see Lady Macbeth she is reading her husband's letter. What do the first 30 lines of scene 5 tell us about her?

   b Does what she says in the rest of the scene change or reinforce your opinion of her? Why?

   c How does Lady Macbeth's contribution to scene 7 add to the picture you are forming of her?

3 Begin a CHARACTER LOG for Lady Macbeth. Bring your other CHARACTER LOGS up to date.

Close study

1 The witches do not appear in these scenes and yet it can be said that the supernatural is very much in evidence.
   - What is this meant to tell us about supernatural powers?
   - Without looking back at the text, can you think of examples

of the influence of the supernatural in this section of the play?
- Now refer to the text. Which scenes and lines show this influence?

2 - At the beginning of scene 7 (lines 1–28) what reasons does Macbeth give for not going ahead with the murder of Duncan? Pick out quotations which outline his reasoning.
   - What arguments does Lady Macbeth use (scene 7 lines 35–59) to get Macbeth to change his mind? How do these arguments show that she knows her husband well? Select quotations which outline her arguments.
   - How does Lady Macbeth's view of the murder of Duncan (scene 7 line 72) contrast with that of Macbeth (scene 7 line 20)?

Writing

1 Write Duncan's diary entries for:
   - the day of Cawdor's execution, when he names Malcolm as his successor and invites himself to Macbeth's castle
   - the day of his arrival at Macbeth's castle. What are his opinions of Macbeth and Lady Macbeth?

2 Look at the beginning of scene 6, when Lady Macbeth enters. Then think about how she behaves in this scene and the next. What is she thinking at the beginning of scene 6? Imagine you are doing a modern picture story of the play. Write the contents of a series of thought bubbles for her for scenes 6 and 7.

3 Lady Macbeth can be a charming hostess (scene 6), but there is obviously a much darker side to her character (scene 5), and a forceful one (scene 7). It is difficult to believe that she has only just developed these characteristics: she must surely have shown signs of unusual behaviour, and perhaps bossiness, before.

  A newly-promoted officer in Macbeth's army, and his wife, were invited to dine with the Macbeths some weeks before the battles referred to in scenes 1 and 2 of the play. They had a pleasant enough evening, but both formed definite opinions about their host and, especially, their hostess. The mothers of both the officer and the officer's wife were very proud that the two of them were to be guests of the famous Macbeths, and they had insisted on being told immediately what the Macbeths were really like. As the officer or the officer's wife, write a letter to your mother about Macbeth and Lady Macbeth, and your evening together.

Quiz

Who said the following, and to whom?
1 'Fair and noble hostess,
   We are your guest tonight'
2 'look like th' innocent flower,
   But be the serpent under't'
3 'Bring forth men-children only'

Who said the following, and about whom?
4 'Nothing in his life
   Became him like the leaving it'
5 'Art not without ambition, but without
   The illness should attend it'
6 'Hath borne his faculties so meek, hath been
   So clear in his great office'

Who said the following, when, and about what?
7 'Would thou hadst less deserved'
8 'The Prince of Cumberland – that is a step,
   On which I must fall down, or else o'erleap'
9 'We will proceed no further in this business'
10 'When you durst do it, then you were a man'

Banquo and his son, Fleance, are on their way to bed
having just left Duncan. They meet Macbeth, and Banquo
broaches the subject of the witches.

How goes the night...?: What time is it?
heard the clock: (anachronism)
husbandry: thrift, economy
candles: stars (see Act 1 scene 4 line 50 and Act 1 scene 5
    lines 50–53)
that too: possibly a sword-belt or a cloak
heavy summons: deep tiredness
would not: do not want to
Merciful powers...repose: you angels who drive away evil
    spirits, stop my nightmares
largess: gifts, usually of money
offices: servants' quarters
diamond: (the diamond was regarded as a charm against
    witchcraft and nightmares)
withal: with especially
shut up: gone to bed
Being unprepared...wrought: because we were unprepared,
    our wish to entertain freely was limited

Act two

Scene **1**

A courtyard in the castle

Enter BANQUO, *and* FLEANCE *bearing a torch before him*

BANQUO	How goes the night, boy?
FLEANCE	The moon is down; I have not heard the clock.
BANQUO	And she goes down at twelve.
FLEANCE	I take't, 'tis later, sir.
BANQUO	Hold, take my sword. There's husbandry in heaven,
	Their candles are all out. Take thee that too.
	A heavy summons lies like lead upon me,
	And yet I would not sleep. Merciful powers,
	Restrain in me the cursed thoughts that nature
	Gives way to in repose. Give me my sword.

Enter MACBETH, *and a* SERVANT *with a torch*

	Who's there?	10
MACBETH	A friend.	
BANQUO	What sir, not yet at rest? The king's a-bed.	
	He hath been in unusual pleasure, and	
	Sent forth great largess to your offices.	
	This diamond he greets your wife withal,	
	By the name of most kind hostess, and shut up	
	In measureless content.	
MACBETH	Being unprepared,	
	Our will became the servant to defect,	
	Which else should free have wrought.	
BANQUO	All's well,	
	I dreamt last night of the three Weird Sisters.	20

Macbeth hints that he looks for Banquo's support in
future, but Banquo makes it clear that he will only act
honourably. As soon as Macbeth is alone, he imagines that
he sees a dagger, leading him to Duncan's room.

---

entreat an hour to serve: find a convenient time
would: should
If you...'tis: (deliberate ambiguity, or double meaning, to test
    Banquo:
    1 if you follow my advice when we talk
    2 if you will support me when the time comes)
honour: rewards
none: (no honour)
augment it: gain higher status
still keep...counselled: if I can keep my heart free from guilt
    and my loyalty unquestioned then I shall listen to you
the bell: (a pre-arranged signal)
Is this...hand?: (The turmoil which we have seen in Macbeth's
    mind makes this hallucination believable to the audience.)
Come...thee: (he tries to take hold of the dagger)
fatal: deadly
sensible: capable of being grasped by the senses
heat-oppressed: feverish
yet: still
palpable: touchable
this which now I draw: (he unsheathes his own dagger)
thou marshall'st: you lead
Mine eyes...rest: my eyes deceive me if the other senses are
    right, or else they are correct and more reliable than all the
    other senses
dudgeon: hilt
gouts: drops
There's no such thing: (the vision fades)

To you they have showed some truth.

MACBETH   I think not of them.
Yet when we can entreat an hour to serve,
We would spend it in some words upon that
    business,
If you would grant the time.

BANQUO   At your kind'st leisure.

MACBETH   If you shall cleave to my consent, when 'tis,
It shall make honour for you.

BANQUO   So I lose none
In seeking to augment it, but still keep
My bosom franchised, and allegiance clear,
I shall be counselled.

MACBETH   Good repose the while.

BANQUO   Thanks sir, the like to you.   30

                 [*Exeunt* BANQUO *and* FLEANCE

MACBETH   Go bid thy mistress, when my drink is ready,
She strike upon the bell. Get thee to bed.
                        [*Exit* SERVANT
Is this a dagger which I see before me,
The handle toward my hand? Come let me clutch
    thee.
I have thee not, and yet I see thee still.
Art thou not, fatal vision, sensible
To feeling as to sight? Or art thou but
A dagger of the mind, a false creation,
Proceeding from the heat-oppressed brain?
I see thee yet, in form as palpable   40
As this which now I draw.
Thou marshall'st me the way that I was going,
And such an instrument I was to use.
Mine eyes are made the fools o' th' other senses,
Or else worth all the rest. I see thee still;
And on thy blade and dudgeon gouts of blood,
Which was not so before. There's no such thing.

Macbeth's mind is in turmoil. He hears the signal and goes to commit the murder of Duncan.

It is...eyes: thoughts of murder are playing tricks with my eyes
one half-world: our hemisphere
Nature...sleep: the world sleeps and nightmares abound
curtained: (reference to curtains round a bed; or, eyelids)
Hecate: (pronounced 'Hecket', with the stress on the first syllable) the goddess of witchcraft
offerings: rituals
and withered...his watch: the wolf, who has been on guard, wakes Murder with his call (personification see GLOSSARY page 238)
thus...pace: (Macbeth moves stealthily)
Tarquin: (Tarquin, son of the king of Rome, raped his hostess, Lucretia, in the dead of night)
prate: prattle, tell
And take...with it: the horror will be lessened by breaking the silence and the tension
Words...gives: talking too much will cool the enthusiasm to act

Lady Macbeth has made the preparations for murder, and she awaits her husband's return.

fire: courage (contrast, *'quench'/'fire'*)
Hark! Peace!: (she is startled by a sudden noise, and then relieved when she realizes it is a bird's cry, not a man's)
fatal bellman: (a man was paid to ring a bell outside the condemned cell of Newgate Prison, London, at midnight before an execution)
stern'st: cruellest
He is about it: Macbeth is committing the murder
surfeited grooms: drunken servants
mock their charge: make a mockery of their duty
possets: hot drinks
That death...die: they are on the borders of life and death

It is the bloody business which informs
Thus to mine eyes. Now o'er the one half-world
Nature seems dead, and wicked dreams abuse   50
The curtained sleep; witchcraft celebrates
Pale Hecate's offerings; and withered murder,
Alarumed by his sentinel the wolf,
Whose howl's his watch, thus with his stealthy pace,
With Tarquin's ravishing strides, towards his design
Moves like a ghost. Thou sure and firm-set earth,
Hear not my steps, which way they walk, for fear
Thy very stones prate of my whereabout,
And take the present horror from the time,
Which now suits with it. Whiles I threat, he lives: 60
Words to the heat of deeds too cold breath gives.
                                        [*A bell rings*
I go, and it is done. The bell invites me.
Hear it not Duncan, for it is a knell
That summons thee to heaven or to hell.   [*Exit*

Scene 2

given servants drugs in drink

The same

Enter LADY MACBETH

can't be

L. MACBETH That which hath made them drunk hath made   *stopped*
                me bold; *confidence*
            What hath quenched them hath given me fire. *metaphor*
listen –   Hark! Peace!   *thinks of execution*
            It was the owl that shrieked, the fatal bellman,   *bell*
            Which gives the stern'st good night. He is about it. *eery*
            The doors are open; and the surfeited grooms
            Do mock their charge with snores. I have drugged
                their possets,
            That death and nature do contend about them,
            Whether they live or die.

Macbeth enters, distracted. He has committed the murder and is obsessed with thoughts of damnation.

'tis done: it's all up, finished
Th' attempt...us: if he has tried to kill Duncan and not
    managed to carry it out then we are ruined
sorry: wretched
one: one of the brothers, Malcolm and Donalbain
addressed them: prepared themselves
hangman's: executioner's
Listening: hearing
Consider...deeply: you are reading too much into this

off stage

MACBETH	[*Within*] Who's there? What ho!
L. MACBETH	Alack, I am afraid they have awaked,
	And 'tis done. Th' attempt and not the deed 10
	Confounds us. Hark! I laid their daggers ready,
	He could not miss 'em. Had he not resembled
	My father as he slept, I had done't. *She couldn't do it*

premeditated murder

Duncan like father

   Enter MACBETH

             My husband!

MACBETH	I have done the deed. Didst thou not hear a noise?
L. MACBETH	I heard the owl scream and the crickets cry.
	Did not you speak?
MACBETH	When?
L. MACBETH	Now.
MACBETH	As I descended?
L. MACBETH	Ay.
MACBETH	Hark! Who lies i' th' second chamber?
L. MACBETH	Donalbain.
MACBETH	This is a sorry sight. [*Looks on his hands*
L. MACBETH	A foolish thought, to say a sorry sight.
MACBETH	There's one did laugh in's sleep, and one cried
	'Murder!' 20
	That they did wake each other. I stood and heard
	them.
	But they did say their prayers, and addressed them
	Again to sleep.
L.MACBETH	There are two lodged together.
MACBETH	One cried 'God bless us!' and 'Amen!' the other,
	As they had seen me with these hangman's hands.
	Listening their fear, I could not say 'Amen',
	When they did say 'God bless us!'
L. MACBETH	Consider it not so deeply.
MACBETH	But wherefore could not I pronounce 'Amen'?

DRAMATIC

guilt

Lady Macbeth tells Macbeth to pull himself together. He has brought the daggers away from the murder scene and refuses to take them back. Lady Macbeth takes them. There is a knocking at the castle gate.

But wherefore...my throat: (the inability to say a prayer was thought to be a sign of being bewitched)

These deeds...mad: (But in lines 10–11 Lady Macbeth said it was *not* the deed which would bring ruin!)

so: thought of like that

Methought I heard...no more:

1 a further reference to sleep

2 is the 'voice' some sound which Macbeth interprets as words, or is it his conscience influenced by the prophecies?

sleave: thread of silk

knits up...care: straightens out worries

death of: rest after

sore labour's bath: means of being refreshed after hard work

Balm: comfort

second course: other form (ie we spend our lives either waking or sleeping)

Chief nourisher: meat (the '*second course*' of a meal)

unbend: give way (compare this with Act 1 scene 7 lines 79–80)

brainsickly: with an ill mind ('*brainsickly*' is used scornfully, not sympathetically)

witness: evidence

Infirm of purpose: weak-minded

but as pictures: only representations of the living person

eye of childhood: eyes of a child

painted devil: picture of the devil

painted: coloured/bloodstained (play on words)

gild: make gold, cover with gilt (gold was regarded as red)

gild (*gilt*)/*guilt*: (play on words)

pluck out mine eyes: (biblical reference to *Matthew 18, 9* – 'if thine eye cause thee to offend, pluck it out')

I had most need of blessing, and 'Amen'
Stuck in my throat.

L. MACBETH   These deeds must not be thought 30
After these ways; so, it will make us mad.

MACBETH Methought I heard a voice cry 'Sleep no more!
Macbeth does murder sleep,' the innocent sleep,
Sleep that knits up the ravelled sleave of care,
The death of each day's life, sore labour's bath,
Balm of hurt minds, great nature's second course,
Chief nourisher in life's feast.

L. MACBETH   What do you mean?

MACBETH Still it cried 'Sleep no more!' to all the house.
Glamis hath murdered sleep, and therefore Cawdor
Shall sleep no more, Macbeth shall sleep no
  more.   40

L. MACBETH Who was it that thus cried? Why worthy Thane,
You do unbend your noble strength, to think
So brainsickly of things. Go get some water,
And wash this filthy witness from your hand.
Why did you bring these daggers from the place?
They must lie there. Go carry them, and smear
The sleepy grooms with blood.

MACBETH   I'll go no more.
I am afraid to think what I have done.
Look on't again I dare not.

L. MACBETH   Infirm of purpose!
Give me the daggers. The sleeping and the dead 50
Are but as pictures. 'Tis the eye of childhood
That fears a painted devil. If he do bleed,
I'll gild the faces of the grooms withal,
For it must seem their guilt.   [Exit. Knock within

MACBETH   Whence is that knocking?
How is't with me, when every noise appals me?
What hands are here? Ha! They pluck out mine
  eyes.

Lady Macbeth returns with blood-stained hands. The knocking at the gate continues and they hurry to put on nightclothes.

Neptune: Roman god of the sea
incarnadine: dye blood-red
Making the green one red: making red the green one (the sea)/making what is green totally red (The First Folio has a comma after *one*.)
entry: gate
Your constancy...unattended: your self-control has deserted you
lest occasion call us: in case we are needed
show us to be watchers: we are seen to be still awake
poorly: dejectedly
To know...myself: I had rather be lost in thought than face the reality of my crime
I would thou couldst: I wish you could!
Exeunt: (Lady Macbeth probably has to lead her husband off)

ACTIVITIES

Keeping track

Scene 1

1 What does Macbeth see, leading him to Duncan's room?
2 What is the signal for Macbeth to commit the murder?

Scene 2

3 How has Lady Macbeth made sure that the guards will not interrupt Macbeth?
4 Whom has Macbeth heard speaking in the room next to Duncan's?

Will all great Neptune's ocean wash this blood
Clean from my hand? No, this my hand will rather
The multitudinous seas incarnadine,
Making the green one red.   60

Enter LADY MACBETH

L. MACBETH   My hands are of your colour; but I shame
To wear a heart so white. [*Knock within*] I hear a
    knocking   *calling him*
                       Cowardly
At the south entry. Retire we to our chamber.
A little water clears us of this deed.
How easy is it then! Your constancy
Hath left you unattended. [*Knock within*] Hark,
    more knocking.
Get on your nightgown, lest occasion call us,
And show us to be watchers. Be not lost
So poorly in your thoughts.

MACBETH   To know my deed, 'twere best not know myself   70
                                          [*Knock within*
Wake Duncan with thy knocking. I would thou
            couldst.   [*Exeunt*

5 Why does Lady Macbeth return to Duncan's room?
6 Why do Macbeth and Lady Macbeth leave hurriedly at the
   end of the scene?

Discussion

1 When Banquo brings up the subject of the witches (scene 1),
   Macbeth says he does not think about them. Why does he lie
   to his old friend? Does Banquo know that he is lying?

2 *'Is this a dagger...?'* (scene 1 line 33)

Is there a dagger? Imagine you are in a rehearsal of this scene. The director wants to know how the dagger is to be represented. Is the actor going to stare into space, or is there going to be a real dagger? Consider the arguments for and against having a dagger. If there is a real dagger, how will it hang in mid-air? Will it make any difference if the dagger is to be represented on film, or for television, rather than in a stage performance?

3 *'ENTER MACBETH*

LADY MACBETH: *My husband!'* (scene 2 line 13)

a Bearing in mind what she has just been saying, how do you think Lady Macbeth speaks these words? Is she anxious, perhaps?

b Bearing in mind what he goes on to say, how do you think Macbeth makes his entrance? Is he triumphant, for instance?

c Some people have said that Lady Macbeth represents Shakespeare's anti-female feelings and that he is using her – the stereotype of a nagging, conniving woman – to hide the violent ambition of Macbeth, his tragic hero. Do you think this interpretation is true?

Drama

1 The whole class learns the lines of Macbeth's anguish and torment (scene 2 lines 32–40). Practise them as a piece of choral speaking. When speaking the lines, experiment with the volume and tone. Some lines could be said by the whole class and others spoken by only a few voices. Try to find and express the sense of anguish that he is suffering at this moment.

Follow up

How would Macbeth explain himself at this moment? Imagine that we could suspend time and give him the opportunity to confess. In small groups, one of you represent the tormented Macbeth, whilst others become confessors or psychologists or friends, who gently question him.

2 '*Infirm of purpose!*' (scene 2 line 49)
Unlike her husband, Lady Macbeth seems to suffer from none
of his reservations and fears. Many people think that she is
more ambitious than Macbeth, and therefore more to blame
than he is. Other people feel that she knows what Macbeth
really wants and has the strength of character to help him when
he weakens:
　　　　'*Thou wouldst be great,*
Art not without ambition, but without
The illness should attend it.' (Act 1 scene 5 lines 18–20)
What is Lady Macbeth thinking at line 52 of Act 2 scene 2?
Hotseat (see page 226) members of your class as Lady
Macbeth, suspended in time, with the bloody daggers in her
hands.

Character

1 '*That my keen knife see not the wound it makes*' (Act 1 scene 5)
'*What cannot you and I perform upon*
Th' unguarded Duncan?' (Act 1 scene 7)
　　　　　　'*Had he not resembled*
My father as he slept, I had done't' (Act 2 scene 2)
　　a What do these quotations show us about Lady Macbeth's
　　　intentions concerning her part in the murder of Duncan?
　　b Does the third quotation show us anything new about her?
　　c Does anything which happens later in the scene make us
　　　surprised that she has been unable to commit the murder
　　　herself?
2 a Macbeth 'sees' a dagger before the murder of Duncan, and
　　　'hears' a voice after it. Does this tell us anything about his
　　　attitude to the murder?
　　b Why is Macbeth so worried that he has been unable to say
　　　'Amen'?
　　c We know that he is a fearless soldier, and yet he refuses to
　　　take the daggers back to Duncan's room. Can you explain
　　　why?
3 Bring your CHARACTER LOGS up to date.

Close study

1 Why do you think Shakespeare wrote scene 2 lines 16–17 as he did? What do the short sentences and the quick exchanges tell us about:
   - the state of mind of Macbeth and Lady Macbeth
   - the atmosphere between them?

2 In scene 2 lines 33–37, Shakespeare describes sleep in various ways. Which one do you think is the best description of the sleep Macbeth has lost? Can you think of other descriptions which would be equally appropriate?

Writing

1 Macbeth's '*Is this a dagger*' speech (scene 1, from line 33) is a key part of the play. Divide it into two.

   a Write a paragraph about lines 33–49 ('*Is this a dagger...to mine eyes*'), in which you say what Macbeth is doing, and what these lines show us about his state of mind.

   b Write a paragraph about lines 49–60 ('*Now o'er...suits with it*'), in which you say how appropriate the imagery is to both the deed Macbeth is about to do, and the way he feels about doing it.

2 How does Fleance come to be at Macbeth's castle? (Does he follow his father everywhere? How has he heard about this occasion? Is his mother with him?) In 25–30 words say why you think he is there and compare your answer with others in the class. Which is the most believable explanation?

Quiz

Who said the following, and to whom?

1 'I dreamt last night of the three Weird Sisters.
   To you they have showed some truth'
2 'Macbeth shall sleep no more'
3 'A little water clears us of this deed'

Who said the following, and about whom?

4 'Whiles I threat, he lives'
5 'One cried "God bless us!" and "Amen!" the other'
6 'If he do bleed,
   I'll gild the faces of the grooms withal'

Who said the following, when, and about what?

7 'If you shall cleave to my consent, when 'tis,
   It shall make honour for you'
8 'That which hath made them drunk hath made me bold'
9 'A foolish thought, to say a sorry sight'
10 'Get on your nightgown, lest occasion call us,
   And show us to be watchers'

A porter comes to open the gate. He has been drinking and he is annoyed that his rest has been disturbed. He delays opening the gate whilst he pretends to be the porter of hell, admitting imaginary sinners. Macduff and Lennox are at the gate.

---

old: plenty of

Beelzebub: a devil, Satan's second-in-command

Here's a farmer...plenty: (the farmer hoarded corn hoping for a poor harvest so that he would make *plenty* of money. When the harvest was exceptionally good, he killed himself.)

Come in time: come in good time, you are welcome

have napkins...you: bring plenty of handkerchieves

th' other devil's name: Satan (the porter forgets his name)

equivocator: double-talker, a person who uses words capable of two meanings in order to deceive

scales: (of justice)

here's an equivocator...heaven: (Father Garnet – also known as Farmer – was hanged in 1606 for his part in the Gunpowder Plot. At his trial he used equivocation in his defence and so all loyal subjects regarded equivocation as damnable.)

here's an English tailor...hose: (it was an old joke that tailors made up customers' cloth into tight garments and kept the leftover material for themselves. '*French hose*' was wide and full, and the suggestion is that the English tailor has re-shaped it and stolen the extra cloth.)

roast your goose: do for you, as in the modern expression 'cook your goose'; also, heat your smoothing-iron (A tailor's iron was called a 'goose' because of the shape of the handle.)

primrose way...bonfire: attractive path to hell

Anon: just a minute!

remember the porter: (he probably expects a tip!)

carousing: doing some serious drinking

second cock: about 3 o'clock in the morning

Marry: by the virgin Mary (in Shakespeare '*marry*' can mean almost anything which might begin a sentence without adding to the meaning – well/indeed/believe me)

nose-painting: reddening the nose

Lechery: lust

Scene 3

The same

Enter A PORTER. *Knocking within*

PORTER | Here's a knocking indeed! If a man were porter of
hell-gate, he should have old turning the key. [*Knock
within*] Knock, knock, knock. Who's there, i' th'
name of Beelzebub? Here's a farmer that hanged
himself on the expectation of plenty. Come in time;
have napkins enow about you, here you'll sweat
for't. [*Knock within*] Knock, knock. Who's there, i'
th' other devil's name? Faith here's an equivocator,
that could swear in both the scales against either
scale, who committed treason enough for God's   10
sake, yet could not equivocate to heaven. O come in,
equivocator. [*Knock within*] Knock, knock, knock.
Who's there? Faith here's an English tailor come
hither, for stealing out of a French hose. Come in
tailor, here you may roast your goose. [*Knock
within*] Knock, knock. Never at quiet. What are you?
But this place is too cold for hell. I'll devil-porter it
no further. I had thought to have let in some of all
professions, that go the primrose way to th'
everlasting bonfire. [*Knock within*] Anon, anon!   20
I pray you remember the porter.   [*Opens the gate*

Enter MACDUFF *and* LENNOX

MACDUFF | Was it so late, friend, ere you went to bed,
That you do lie so late?

PORTER | Faith sir, we were carousing till the second cock;
and drink, sir, is a great provoker of three things.

MACDUFF | What three things does drink especially provoke?

PORTER | Marry sir, nose-painting, sleep, and urine. Lechery,

Macduff and the porter indulge in banter until Macbeth arrives. Macduff goes to wake Duncan as arranged.

---

it provokes...performance: it makes a man lustful but prevents him from doing anything about it

Therefore much drink...leaves him: too much alcohol is a double-dealer with lust: it creates lust in a man but hinders it; it encourages the man and discourages him; it makes him feel ready for action but unable to act; in the end it tricks him into sleeping and, having put him on his back, it leaves him

giving him the lie: knocking him out/cheating him (play on words)

gave thee the lie: held you down (like a wrestler)

i' the very throat on me: (play on words – drink lay in his throat/to lie in one's throat, or tell a big lie, was a popular expression)

requited: repaid

took up my legs: took my legs away (as in wrestling)/made me lift up my leg (as a dog!) (play on words)

made a shift: managed/repented (put on a hair shirt, *shift*) (play on words)

cast: throw/vomit (play on words)

timely: early

I have...hour: I am nearly late

yet 'tis one: a trouble

The labour...pain: (this was a proverb of the time) when we do what we enjoy it acts as a medicine to trouble

limited service: appointed duty

Goes the king hence: Is the king leaving?

he did appoint so: he said he was

lay: spent the night

as they say: so they say

sir, it provokes, and unprovokes; it provokes the
desire, but it takes away the performance. Therefore
much drink may be said to be an equivocator   30
with lechery; it makes him, and it mars him; it sets
him on, and it takes him off; it persuades him, and
disheartens him; makes him stand to, and not stand
to; in conclusion, equivocates him in a sleep, and,
giving him the lie, leaves him.

MACDUFF   I believe drink gave thee the lie last night.

PORTER   That it did sir, i' the very throat on me; but I
requited him for his lie, and I think, being too
strong for him, though he took up my legs
sometime, yet I made a shift to cast him.   40

MACDUFF   Is thy master stirring?
Our knocking has awaked him, here he comes.

Enter MACBETH

LENNOX   Good morrow, noble sir.
MACBETH   Good morrow, both.

MACDUFF   Is the King stirring, worthy Thane?
MACBETH   Not yet.

MACDUFF   He did command me to call timely on him.
I have almost slipped the hour.

MACBETH   I'll bring you to him.

MACDUFF   I know this is a joyful trouble to you;
But yet 'tis one.

MACBETH   The labour we delight in physics pain.
This is the door.

MACDUFF   I'll make so bold to call,
For 'tis my limited service.   [*Exit* 50

LENNOX   Goes the king hence today?

MACBETH   He does – he did appoint so.

LENNOX   The night has been unruly. Where we lay,
Our chimneys were blown down, and as they say,

Lennox reports strange events in the night. Macduff returns, appalled by Duncan's death, and he tells Lennox and Macbeth to go to see for themselves. Macduff rouses the rest of the house.

Lamentings: wailings

dire combustion: fearful civil unrest

New hatched...time: to be produced by this dreadful state of affairs

obscure bird: owl ('*obscure*' because it is nocturnal)

feverous...shake: shook with an earthquake because it was sick

a rough night: (Does Macbeth agree with Lennox or is he thinking of his own night?)

My young...to it: I am not old but I cannot remember a night like it

Tongue nor...thee: heart cannot conceive and tongue cannot name (Macduff is so distraught that he is not thinking straight)

What's the matter?: what is the matter about which you speak? what is it that you are saying?

Confusion...masterpiece: this is the ultimate in destruction, it could not be worse

sacrilegious...temple: (kings were regarded as appointed by God, and so killing a king was a sacrilegious act; the king's body was the home/house/temple of God's spirit) Biblical references: 'the Lord's anointed' *1 Samuel 24, 10*; the human body was 'the temple of the living God' *2 Corinthians 6, 16*

temple/building: (imagery continued)

Gorgon: snake-haired monster of Greek mythology which turned to stone all who looked at it

alarum-bell: alarm bell, the great bell of the castle

downy: light, of little substance

counterfeit: imitation

great doom's image: picture of Judgement Day

rise up: (on the Day of Judgement the dead will rise up)

sprites: spirits

countenance: face

Lamentings heard i' th' air, strange screams of
    death,
And prophesying with accents terrible,
Of dire combustion, and confused events,
New hatched to the woeful time. The obscure bird
Clamoured the livelong night. Some say, the earth
Was feverous, and did shake.

MACBETH   'Twas a rough night.

LENNOX   My young remembrance cannot parallel   60
A fellow to it.

Enter MACDUFF

MACDUFF   O horror, horror, horror! Tongue nor heart
Cannot conceive nor name thee.

MACBETH, LENNOX   What's the matter?

MACDUFF   Confusion now hath made his masterpiece.
Most sacrilegious murder hath broken ope
The Lord's anointed temple, and stole thence
The life o' th' building!

MACBETH   What is't you say – the life?

LENNOX   Mean you his Majesty?

MACDUFF   Approach the chamber, and destroy your sight
With a new Gorgon. Do not bid me speak.   70
See, and then speak yourselves.
                    [*Exeunt* MACBETH *and* LENNOX
                    Awake, awake!
Ring the alarum-bell. Murder and treason!
Banquo and Donalbain! Malcolm awake!
Shake off this downy sleep, death's counterfeit,
And look on death itself! Up, up and see
The great doom's image! Malcolm! Banquo!
As from your graves rise up, and walk like sprites,
To countenance this horror!   [*Bell rings*

Enter LADY MACBETH

L. MACBETH   What's the business,

The news of Duncan's murder is given to Banquo, Lady Macbeth, Malcolm and Donalbain. It is assumed that Duncan's guards are responsible.

trumpet...parley: (the bell would usually be rung in times of war)

The repetition...fell: If I were to tell a woman it would kill her as she heard it

chance: mischance, calamity

nothing serious in mortality: human life is not important

toys: trifles, things of no consequence

Renown and grace: fame and honour

The wine...brag of: the best things in life are taken and only the dregs ('*lees*') are left for this world to boast about

vault: wine cellar/burial chamber/earth, with the vaulted (arched) roof of the heavens

Had I...brag of: (Is Macbeth speaking about Duncan, making his '*griefs and clamour roar*' Act 1 scene 7 line 78? Or is it a heartfelt summary of his own guilt?)

O! by whom?: (Is this a more natural response than Lady Macbeth's?)

badged: marked (servants wore the badge of their master)

They stared...distracted: (they were recovering from the effects of the drugged possets)

That such a hideous trumpet calls to parley   80
The sleepers of the house? Speak, speak.

MACDUFF   O gentle lady,
'Tis not for you to hear what I can speak;
The repetition in a woman's ear
Would murder as it fell.

Enter BANQUO

                              O Banquo, Banquo,
Our royal master's murdered.

L. MACBETH   Woe, alas!
What, in our house?

BANQUO   Too cruel anywhere.
Dear Duff, I prithee contradict thyself,
And say it is not so.

Enter MACBETH *and* LENNOX

MACBETH   Had I but died an hour before this chance,
I had lived a blessed time; for from this instant,   90
There's nothing serious in mortality;
All is but toys. Renown and grace is dead,
The wine of life is drawn, and the mere lees
Is left this vault to brag of.

Enter MALCOLM *and* DONALBAIN

DONALBAIN   What is amiss?

MACBETH   You are, and do not know't.
The spring, the head, the fountain of your blood
Is stopped, the very source of it is stopped.

MACDUFF   Your royal father's murdered.

MALCOLM   O, by whom?

LENNOX   Those of his chamber, as it seemed, had done't.
Their hands and faces were all badged with
        blood,   100
So were their daggers, which unwiped we found
Upon their pillows. They stared, and were distracted,

Macbeth announces that he has killed the guards and says that his love for Duncan drove him to do it. Lady Macbeth collapses and is taken for treatment. Banquo begins to take charge of the situation.

---

fury: frenzy
amazed: frantic
temperate: level-headed
The expedition...reason: the overwhelming need to express my love was stronger than my commonsense, which would have held me back
expedition: rush
pauser: that which makes one pause
laced: decorated
golden blood: (gold was regarded as being red)
breach in nature: break in (the wall of) life
ruin: death
wasteful: destructive
steeped: dyed
Unmannerly breeched: indecently clothed
make's: make his
Who can be...known?: (It has been said that for a man of action like Macbeth the language is artificial, 'forced')
Help...ho!: (Is this a diversionary tactic; or is she overcome by Macbeth's reconstruction of the murder scene?)
Look to: look after
Why do...ours?: Why are we silent when this matter concerns us most?
our fate...seize us: someone could be watching us, waiting for the opportunity to do the same to us
auger-hole: spy-hole
brewed: ready for pouring out
upon the foot of motion: ready for expression
naked frailties: (only Macduff and Lennox are dressed)
question: discuss
Fears...shake us: fears and suspicions disturb us
undivulged pretence: hidden plot

	No man's life was to be trusted with them.
MACBETH	O yet I do repent me of my fury,
	That I did kill them.
MACDUFF	Wherefore did you so?
MACBETH	Who can be wise, amazed, temperate and furious,
	Loyal and neutral, in a moment? No man.
	The expedition of my violent love
	Outran the pauser, reason. Here lay Duncan,
	His silver skin laced with his golden blood, 110
	And his gashed stabs looked like a breach in nature
	For ruin's wasteful entrance; there the murderers,
	Steeped in the colours of their trade, their daggers
	Unmannerly breeched with gore. Who could refrain,
	That had a heart to love, and in that heart
	Courage to make's love known?
L. MACBETH	Help me hence, ho! [*Faints*
MACDUFF	Look to the lady.
MALCOLM	[*Aside to* DONALBAIN] Why do we hold our tongues,
	That most may claim this argument for ours?
DONALBAIN	[*Aside to* MALCOLM] What should be spoken
	Here where our fate, hid in an auger-hole, 120
	May rush and seize us? Let's away; our tears
	Are not yet brewed.
MALCOLM	[*Aside to* DONALBAIN] Nor our strong sorrow
	Upon the foot of motion.
BANQUO	Look to the lady.
	[LADY MACBETH *is carried out*
	And when we have our naked frailties hid,
	That suffer in exposure, let us meet,
	And question this most bloody piece of work,
	To know it further. Fears and scruples shake us.
	In the great hand of God I stand, and thence
	Against the undivulged pretence I fight
	Of treasonous malice.

They all join Banquo in swearing an oath to the cause of right. Whilst the others are dressing, Malcolm and Donalbain decide to flee – to England and Ireland, respectively.

briefly: quickly
put on manly readiness: get dressed/get ready for action
consort: associate
office: action
Our separated...safer: we shall be safer in future if we split up
Where we...bloody: here we cannot tell what people are really thinking; the more closely related the murderer is to us, the more likely is he to kill us
This murderous...aim: (the imagery is of Murder being an arrow fired into the air; it has not yet landed *('lighted')* so other murders will be committed)
dainty of leave-taking: particular about saying goodbye
shift: slip
warrant in: justification for
steals: robs *('theft')*/sneaks away
steals itself: takes itself off/*'steels itself'*: hardens itself, preparing for the worst

Ross and an old man begin discussing the strange events in nature of the previous night.

Threescore and ten: seventy (biblical reference)
sore: dreadful
Hath trifled former knowings: has made previous experiences seem trifling
father: (a form of address used for a much older man)
heavens: sky
act: deeds
bloody stage: earth, the scene of bloodshed
heavens/stage: (theatrical reference, see page vi)

MACDUFF	And so do I.
ALL	So all. 130
MACBETH	Let's briefly put on manly readiness,
	And meet i' th' hall together.
ALL	Well contented.

[Exeunt all but MALCOLM *and* DONALBAIN

MALCOLM	What will you do? Let's not consort with them.
	To show an unfelt sorrow is an office
	Which the false man does easy. I'll to England.
DONALBAIN	To Ireland I. Our separated fortune
	Shall keep us both the safer. Where we are,
	There's daggers in men's smiles; the near in blood,
	The nearer bloody.
MALCOLM	This murderous shaft that's shot
	Hath not yet lighted, and our safest way 140
	Is to avoid the aim. Therefore to horse,
	And let us not be dainty of leave-taking,
	But shift away. There's warrant in that theft
	Which steals itself, when there's no mercy left.

[Exeunt

Scene 4

Outside the castle

Enter ROSS *and an* OLD MAN

OLD MAN	Threescore and ten I can remember well,
	Within the volume of which time I have seen
	Hours dreadful, and things strange; but this sore night
	Hath trifled former knowings.
ROSS	Ha, good father,
	Thou seest the heavens, as troubled with man's act,
	Threatens his bloody stage: by th' clock 'tis day,

Ross and the old man add to the description which Lennox has already given. Macduff confirms that the guards were responsible for Duncan's death, and says that Malcolm and Donalbain are suspected of arranging it.

lamp: sun

predominance: superior influence

Is't night's... kiss it? Is it because night is more powerful, or because day is ashamed to look on the murder that it is dark now when it should be light?

towering: flying very high

pride of place: highest point of flight

hawked at: swooped on like a hawk (owls usually fly close to the ground)

minions: choicest

Turned wild in nature: became uncontrollable

Contending 'gainst obedience: disregarding orders

How goes the world: how are things?/what news? (Macduff has come from the meeting arranged at the end of the previous scene)

What good could they pretend?: What did they hope to get out of it?

suborned: bribed

'Gainst nature still: another example of the unnatural!

Thriftless: thoughtless, not caring for the future

ravin up: swallow, devour

Thine own life's means: the means of giving you your life – your father

And yet dark night strangles the travelling lamp.
Is't night's predominance, or the day's shame,
That darkness does the face of earth entomb,
When living light should kiss it?

OLD MAN   'Tis unnatural,   10
Even like the deed that's done. On Tuesday last,
A falcon towering in her pride of place
Was by a mousing owl hawked at, and killed.

ROSS   And Duncan's horses – a thing most strange and
             certain –
Beauteous and swift, the minions of their race,
Turned wild in nature, broke their stalls, flung out,
Contending 'gainst obedience, as they would make
War with mankind.

OLD MAN   'Tis said they eat each other.

ROSS   They did so, to th' amazement of mine eyes
That looked upon't. Here comes the good
             Macduff.   20

Enter MACDUFF

How goes the world sir, now?

MACDUFF   Why, see you not?

ROSS   Is't known who did this more than bloody deed?

MACDUFF Those that Macbeth hath slain.

ROSS   Alas the day,
What good could they pretend?

MACDUFF   They were suborned.
Malcolm and Donalbain, the King's two sons,
Are stolen away and fled, which puts upon them
Suspicion of the deed.

ROSS   'Gainst nature still.
Thriftless ambition, that will ravin up
Thine own life's means! Then 'tis most like
The sovereignty will fall upon Macbeth.   30

Macduff tells them that Macbeth has been named to
succeed Duncan, but he (Macduff) will not attend the
coronation.

named: elected
Scone: (where Scottish kings were crowned – pronounced
Skoon)
Colme-kill: (the royal burial-ground on the island of Iona)
Fife: (site of Macduff's castle)
thither: to Scone
Well/well: (ironic repetition of Ross's '*well*')
Lest our...new: for fear that the old reign will prove to have
been more comfortable than the new one (imagery of
clothing)
benison: blessing

ACTIVITIES

Keeping track

Scene 3

1 Who are the visitors and what have they come for?
2 Who discovers the body?
3 What has happened to the guards?
4 What do Malcolm and Donalbain decide to do?

Scene 4

5 Who is suspected of being involved in Duncan's murder?
Why?
6 Who has been named as Duncan's successor?

MACDUFF	He is already named, and gone to Scone
	To be invested.
ROSS	Where is Duncan's body?
MACDUFF	Carried to Colme-kill,
	The sacred storehouse of his predecessors,
	And guardian of their bones.
ROSS	Will you to Scone?
MACDUFF	No cousin, I'll to Fife.
ROSS	Well, I will thither.
MACDUFF	Well, may you see things well done there. Adieu.
	Lest our old robes sit easier than our new!
ROSS	Farewell, father.
OLD MAN	God's benison go with you, and with those
	That would make good of bad, and friends of
	foes. 40
	[*Exeunt*

Discussion

1 a Some say that the first part of scene 3 lines 1–40 is a comic
interlude, giving the audience relief after the tension of the
previous scene, and before the renewed tension of the rest
of this scene. Others say that lines 1–40 emphasize the evil
of Macbeth's actions. Can you see both sides of the
argument? What do you think Shakespeare's purpose was?

b Are lines 1–40 an example of irony or dramatic irony? (If
you are not sure what these terms mean, there is an
explanation of them in the GLOSSARY on page 238.)

2 Read again scene 3 lines 89–97. Is Macbeth merely putting on
an act here, or is it possible that he can really mean what he

says? Did he say anything at the end of the previous scene
which might give us a guide to his feelings here?

3 '*God's benison go with you, and with those
   That would make good of bad, and friends of foes.*' (scene 4
   lines 39–40) This could mean either:
   a Bless those who want to put things right and convert our
      enemies, or
   b Bless those who see good in evil deeds, and are willing to
      make friends with our enemies. It has been suggested
      that the old man thinks that Ross is a person who looks
      after his own interests. If this is so:
      • which meaning applies, a or b?
      • how do these words fit the definition of irony?

Drama

1 '*O, horror, horror, horror!*' (scene 3 line 62)
   This is a very difficult line to deliver, but it is essential that
   the actor avoids making it too melodramatic. In groups of
   eight or nine try to demonstrate the horror of the moment.
   Apart from Lennox, Macbeth, Macduff and the Porter,
   who are present, you could also portray the reactions of
   Lady Macbeth, Malcolm, Donalbain and Ross, who, if they
   do not hear the actual words, hear them in their minds.

   You can use the conventions of FREEZE! and FORUM
   THEATRE (see pages 227–228) to explore this moment of
   high tension.

2 Reporters are going to interview the people who were at
   Macbeth's castle at the time of the king's murder. Some of
   you can be those people and the rest of you could work in
   twos and threes as reporters. Decide which sort of
   newspaper you work for. Interview as many of the
   important people as you can.

   You might find it helpful to spend some time preparing
   for this. The reporters need to think of some good
   questions, and equally the witnesses need to think of some
   good answers; some of them need to agree on their versions
   of events!

3 As a whole class, re-enact Duncan's funeral. Where will people stand? Who is there and who is missing? Find some way to indicate their absence.

Character

1 How do you see the character of the porter? To begin with, is he tall and thin or short and fat, perhaps? Is he always like this, or do we see him on a good/bad day? Is he a quick-witted scrounger or a dull drunkard? If you were casting the role today, which modern actor (or character if you do not know the actor's name) would you choose to play the part?

2 How does Macduff react to:
   • Duncan's death
   • Macbeth's being named king?
   What do you think might happen between Macbeth and Macduff in the future?

3 What do we learn of Banquo from scene 3 lines 124–130?

4 When Lady Macbeth is 'told' of Duncan's death, she says, '*What, in our house?*' Is this a carefully-prepared response which would be the obvious thing for any hostess to say; or is it a mistake which might arouse suspicion? Has she just lost concentration for a moment or is the strain beginning to tell?

5 Bring your CHARACTER LOGS up to date.

Close study

1 Read again scene 3 lines 54–59 and scene 4 lines 1–20. Why are these descriptions included? Do the events described have anything to do with the plot of the play? Would the audience of Shakespeare's day think that they were distractions? Why are there so many references to birds and beasts?

2 Lady Macbeth 'faints' (scene 3 line 116). It is suggested that she does this because Macbeth's speech (lines 106–116) is so obviously contrived and artificial that she feels she must distract attention from him. Can you identify what is worrying her? First read aloud scene 3 lines 89–94, then read aloud scene 3 lines 106–116.

a Does the second speech sound 'artificial' at all? Does it seem as if Macbeth is not speaking from the heart, but for effect? Can you pinpoint particular words or phrases which might cause Lady Macbeth some concern?

b Perhaps the original suggestion (that Lady Macbeth is only pretending to faint) seems nonsense to you; perhaps you think that she really does faint. If that is so, can you explain why Lady Macbeth, who has been so strong up to this point, should suddenly show physical weakness?

Writing

1 Macbeth will need a new crest, or badge, now that he is king. In groups of four or six you are going to design **two** crests.

- Half of you are commissioned by Macbeth. You will produce a design which he can bear proudly, consisting of a shield with a crown on top and a motto underneath. The shield can be divided into two, three or four sections, each containing a representation of some feature of Macbeth's life which he would want to display as King of Scotland. There might be an emblem to show that he is proud to be Scottish, for instance; and another to show his prowess as a soldier.

- The other half of the group will produce a crest which portrays the real Macbeth. It might well contain some of the same features as the 'official' version (after all, it cannot be denied that he is an outstanding soldier) but it will also be very different. The basic pattern of shield, crown and motto will be the same for both crests.

2 There cannot be many bigger stories for a journalist than the assassination of a king. You are a reporter working for a Scottish newspaper in 1040. The death of Duncan, and related stories (Macbeth's succession and the disappearance of Malcolm and Donalbain, for instance), will probably occupy the whole of the front page. Decide the type of newspaper you are writing for. Write your newspaper's front page with headlines and sub-headings as necessary.

Quiz

Who said the following, and to whom?

1 '*O gentle lady,*
  'Tis not for you to hear what I can speak'
2 '*The spring, the head, the fountain of your blood*
  Is stopped, the very source of it is stopped'
3 '*Our separated fortune*
  Shall keep us both the safer'

Who said the following, and about whom?

4 '*He did command me call timely on him*'
5 '*Their hands and faces were all badged with blood*'
6 '*He is already named, and gone to Scone*
  To be invested'

Who said the following, when, and about what?

7 '*Had I but died an hour before this chance,*
  I had lived a blessed time'
8 '*Who can be wise, amazed, temperate and furious,*
  Loyal and neutral, in a moment?'
9 '*This murderous shaft that's shot*
  Hath not yet lighted'
10 '*'Tis said they ate each other*'

Macbeth is king, and Banquo suspects him of foul play.
Macbeth and Lady Macbeth make a great show of inviting
Banquo to a formal banquet.

play'dst: plotted
It: the succession
stand in thy posterity: remain in your family
root: beginning, source
them: the witches
shine: show favour
verities: truths
oracles: prophets
But hush, no more: (he is beginning to be tempted – like
   Macbeth – but dismisses such thoughts)
all-thing unbecoming: totally unfitting
solemn: formal
I'll: (the invitation is personal)
to the which: your command
my duties...knit: I am bound with an unbreakable tie to do
   my duty (This was the usual, formal response from a subject
   to a king in these circumstances.)
We: (Macbeth uses the royal plural)

Act three

Scene 1

The palace at Forres

Enter BANQUO

BANQUO   Thou hast it now, King, Cawdor, Glamis, all,
              As the weird women promised, and I fear
              Thou play'dst most foully for't; yet it was said
              It should not stand in thy posterity,
              But that myself should be the root and father
              Of many kings. If there come truth from them,
              As upon thee Macbeth, their speeches shine,
              Why by the verities on thee made good
              May they not be my oracles as well,
              And set me up in hope? But hush, no more.   10

              Sennet sounded. Enter MACBETH *as king,* LADY
              MACBETH *as queen,* LENNOX, ROSS, LORDS, LADIES,
              and ATTENDANTS

MACBETH   Here's our chief guest.

L. MACBETH   If he had been forgotten,
              It had been as a gap in our great feast,
              And all-thing unbecoming.

MACBETH   Tonight we hold a solemn supper, sir,
              And I'll request your presence.

BANQUO   Let your Highness
              Command upon me, to the which my duties
              Are with a most indissoluble tie
              For ever knit.

MACBETH   Ride you this afternoon?

BANQUO   Ay, my good lord.   20

MACBETH   We should have else desired your good advice,

Banquo is going riding with Fleance before the banquet.
Macbeth asks to be left alone so that he will appreciate
company later. He admits that Banquo worries him.

'Twixt this: between now
Go not...better: if my horse is not fast enough
twain: two
Fail not: do not miss
bloody cousins: Malcolm and Donalbain – Macbeth has
    branded them killers
bestowed: lodged
parricide: patricide, murder of their father
strange invention: stories of Macbeth's guilt
cause: matters
Craving us jointly: requiring our joint attention
Hie: hurry
our time does call upon's: it is time we went
to make...welcome: so that you will enjoy our (i.e. my)
    company all the more
While: until
Sirrah: a term used when addressing someone socially inferior
Attend...pleasure?: are those men waiting?
without: outside
To be thus...thus: to be king is worth nothing unless I am safe
Stick: (like daggers)
in his...feared: he has a king-like quality which has to be
    greatly respected

> Which still hath been both grave and prosperous,
> In this day's council; but we'll take tomorrow.
> Is't far you ride?

BANQUO   As far, my lord, as will fill up the time
> 'Twixt this and supper. Go not my horse the better,
> I must become a borrower of the night
> For a dark hour or twain.

MACBETH   Fail not our feast.

BANQUO   My lord, I will not.

MACBETH   We hear our bloody cousins are bestowed   30
> In England and in Ireland, not confessing
> Their cruel parricide, filling their hearers
> With strange invention. But of that tomorrow,
> When therewithal we shall have cause of state
> Craving us jointly. Hie you to horse. Adieu,
> Till you return at night. Goes Fleance with you?

BANQUO   Ay my good lord; our time does call upon's.

MACBETH   I wish your horses swift, and sure of foot;
> And so I do commend you to their backs.
> Farewell.   [*Exit* BANQUO   40
> Let every man be master of his time
> Till seven at night; to make society
> The sweeter welcome, we will keep ourself
> Till supper-time alone. While then, God be with
> you!
>   [*Exeunt all but* MACBETH *and an* ATTENDANT

> Sirrah, a word with you. Attend those men
> Our pleasure?

ATTENDANT   They are, my lord, without the palace gate.

MACBETH   Bring them before us.   [*Exit* ATTENDANT
>   To be thus is nothing,
> But to be safely thus. Our fears in Banquo
> Stick deep, and in his royalty of nature   50
> Reigns that which would be feared. 'Tis much he
> dares,

Macbeth is bitter that, if the witches' prophecies come true, he has killed Duncan for the benefit of Banquo's descendants. He speaks with two murderers, assuring them that their misfortunes are Banquo's fault.

---

to that dauntless temper: in addition to the fearless quality
wisdom: commonsense
Genius is rebuked: guardian spirit is checked (i.e. Banquo has a stronger spirit than Macbeth, whose guilt is a weakening force)
chid: reproached
fruitless crown and **barren sceptre**: (Macbeth has no son)
gripe: grip
with: by
unlineal: not of my line, descendants
filed: defiled
rancours: bitterness
eternal jewel: immortal soul
common enemy of man: devil
seed: children
list: tournament, scene of contest
champion...utterance: challenge me in a fight to the death
under fortune: below what you deserve
made good: showed
passed in probation: proved
borne in hand: tricked
crossed: thwarted
instruments: means

And to that dauntless temper of his mind,
He hath a wisdom that doth guide his valour
To act in safety. There is none but he
Whose being I do fear; and under him
My Genius is rebuked, as it is said
Mark Antony's was by Caesar. He chid the sisters,
When first they put the name of king upon me,
And bade them speak to him. Then, prophet-like,
They hailed him father to a line of kings.   60
Upon my head they placed a fruitless crown,
And put a barren sceptre in my gripe,
Thence to be wrenched with an unlineal hand,
No son of mine succeeding. If't be so,
For Banquo's issue have I filed my mind,
For them the gracious Duncan have I murdered,
Put rancours in the vessel of my peace
Only for them, and mine eternal jewel
Given to the common enemy of man,
To make them kings, the seed of Banquo kings.   70
Rather than so, come fate, into the list,
And champion me to th' utterance. Who's there?

Enter SERVANT, *with two* MURDERERS

Now go to the door, and stay there till we call.
                                        [*Exit* SERVANT

Was it not yesterday we spoke together?

1ST M.   It was, so please your Highness.

MACBETH   Well then, now
Have you considered of my speeches? Know
That it was he in the times past which held you
So under fortune, which you thought had been
Our innocent self. This I made good to you
In our last conference, passed in probation with
    you,   80
How you were borne in hand, how crossed; the
    instruments;

Macbeth urges the murderers to take revenge on Banquo and his family. He tries to persuade them that becoming assassins will prove that they are 'real' men.

---

wrought with: used
half a soul: half-wit
notion crazed: crazy mind, imbecile
Our point of: the point of our
let this go: 'this' = what Banquo has done
so gospelled: so religious
To pray...man: (biblical reference – 'Love your enemies... and pray for them that persecute you' *Matthew 5, 44*)
issue: children (it is important to Macbeth that Fleance should not be able to carry on Banquo's family tree!)
beggared yours: made your children beggars
We are men: (ironically, this is scorned by Macbeth in lines 92–103, as Lady Macbeth taunted him for ' *I dare do all that may become a man*' Act 1 scene 7 line 46)
liege: lord (from the same root word as 'allegiance')
catalogue: list
shoughs: shaggy dogs
water-rugs: rough water-dogs
demi-wolves: cross-breeds
clept: called
valued file: more detailed list
subtle: clever
housekeeper: guard-dog
bounteous: generous
closed: set, enclosed
Particular...alike: special name apart from 'dog'
station in the file: place in the list
Not i' th' worst rank of manhood: (but could anything be worse than what Macbeth is suggesting?)
execution...off: (play on words) '*execution*' killing/carrying out the business; '*takes...off*' takes away/kills
in his life: as long as he is alive
the vile...world: I have taken so many knocks that I can take no more and I don't care what I do to get revenge
tugged: pulled about

Who wrought with them; and all things else that
    might
To half a soul and to a notion crazed
Say 'Thus did Banquo.'

1ST M.   You made it known to us.

MACBETH   I did so; and went further, which is now
Our point of second meeting. Do you find
Your patience so predominant in your nature,
That you can let this go? Are you so gospelled
To pray for this good man, and for his issue,
Whose heavy hand hath bowed you to the grave, 90
And beggared yours for ever?

1ST M.   We are men, my liege.

MACBETH   Ay, in the catalogue ye go for men,
As hounds, and greyhounds, mongrels, spaniels, curs,
Shoughs, water-rugs, and demi-wolves are clept
All by the name of dogs; the valued file
Distinguishes the swift, the slow, the subtle,
The housekeeper, the hunter, every one
According to the gift which bounteous nature
Hath in him closed, whereby he does receive
Particular addition, from the bill   100
That writes them all alike; and so of men.
Now if you have a station in the file,
Not i' th' worst rank of manhood, say't,
And I will put that business in your bosoms,
Whose execution takes your enemy off,
Grapples you to the heart and love of us,
Who wear our health but sickly in his life,
Which in his death were perfect.

2ND M.   I am one, my liege,
Whom the vile blows and buffets of the world
Have so incensed, that I am reckless what   110
I do to spite the world.

1ST M.   And I another
So weary with disasters, tugged with fortune,

The murderers agree to kill Banquo and Fleance.

set: stake
mend: improve
bloody distance: (fighting imagery) space between swordsmen
in such...of life: he is so close that every minute he lives he is
    threatening my heart/life
barefaced: open, undisguised
avouch: justify
bid my...it: simply say it is what I want
For: because of
but wail: but must bewail, mourn
do make love: call upon
common: public
sundry weighty: various important
Acquaint you...time: make known to you precisely the ideal
    time
on't: of the murder
something: some distance
always thought: always bear in mind
I require a clearness: I must be clear of suspicion
rubs nor botches: rough spots nor blemishes
absence: death
material: important
embrace: share
Resolve yourselves apart: go away and prepare yourselves
anon: soon
I'll call...straight: I'll join you straight away
abide within: wait in an inner room

	That I would set my life on any chance,
	To mend it, or be rid on't.
MACBETH	Both of you
	Know Banquo was your enemy.
BOTH M.	True my lord.

MACBETH   So is he mine; and in such bloody distance
That every minute of his being thrusts
Against my near'st of life; and though I could
With barefaced power sweep him from my sight,
And bid my will avouch it, yet I must not,   120
For certain friends that are both his and mine,
Whose loves I may not drop, but wail his fall
Who I myself struck down. And thence it is,
That I to your assistance do make love,
Masking the business from the common eye
For sundry weighty reasons.

2ND M.   We shall, my lord,
Perform what you command us.

1ST M.   Though our lives –

MACBETH   Your spirits shine through you. Within this hour at
                most,
I will advise you where to plant yourselves,
Acquaint you with the perfect spy o' th' time,   130
The moment on't, for't must be done tonight,
And something from the palace; always thought
That I require a clearness: and with him –
To leave no rubs nor botches in the work –
Fleance his son, that keeps him company,
Whose absence is no less material to me
Than is his father's, must embrace the fate
Of that dark hour. Resolve yourselves apart,
I'll come to you anon.

BOTH M.   We are resolved, my lord.
MACBETH   I'll call upon you straight; abide within.   140

[*Exeunt* MURDERERS

Lady Macbeth is as uneasy about their position as Macbeth is, but she presents a different face to her husband.

Is Banquo gone from Court?: (An innocent question? A reminder to the audience?)

Nought's had...content: nothing has been gained, all has been lost, when we have got what we wanted but do not have peace of mind (see Act 3 scene 1 lines 48–49)

that which we destroy: our victim, Duncan

doubtful: full of fear

'Tis safer...joy: (the rhyming couplet marks the end of this train of thought)

sorriest fancies: saddest images

using: accompanying

Things without...regard: what cannot be changed should be ignored

scorched: slashed, wounded

close: heal up

whilst our...tooth: whilst our weak attempt to kill it off means that we are as threatened as we were before

the frame...disjoint: the universe fall to pieces

both the worlds: heaven and earth

Ere: before

affliction: suffering

shake: (with terror) '*Macbeth does murder sleep*' (see Act 2 scene 2 line 33)

Better be...further: (see lines 6–7)

It is concluded. Banquo, thy soul's flight,
If it find heaven, must find it out tonight.   [*Exit*

Scene 2

The palace at Forres

Enter LADY MACBETH *and a* SERVANT

L. MACBETH   Is Banquo gone from Court?

SERVANT   Ay madam, but returns again tonight.

L. MACBETH   Say to the King, I would attend his leisure
For a few words.

SERVANT   Madam I will.   [*Exit*

L. MACBETH   Nought's had, all's spent,
Where our desire is got without content.
'Tis safer to be that which we destroy,
Than by destruction dwell in doubtful joy.

Enter MACBETH

How now my lord? Why do you keep alone,
Of sorriest fancies your companions making,
Using those thoughts which should indeed have
        died   10
With them they think on? Things without all
        remedy
Should be without regard: what's done is done.

MACBETH   We have scorched the snake, not killed it:
She'll close, and be herself, whilst our poor malice
Remains in danger of her former tooth.
But let the frame of things disjoint, both the worlds
        suffer,
Ere we will eat our meal in fear, and sleep
In the affliction of these terrible dreams
That shake us nightly. Better be with the dead,

Lady Macbeth urges her husband to put the past behind him. Macbeth hints that he has a plan in hand which will be carried out that evening. He will not give Lady Macbeth the details but he says that she will approve.

to gain...to peace: to secure our own peace (by satisfying our ambition) we sent him to his peace (of death)
on the torture...to lie: (as on a rack of torture)
ecstasy: frenzy
steel: sword, dagger
Malice domestic: civil war
levy: army
Gentle: noble
sleek o'er...looks: make pleasant your harsh appearance
Let your...to: remember particularly
Present him eminence: honour him as chief guest
Unsafe...streams: we are unsafe at the moment and so we must keep our titles (ourselves) clean (free from enmity or envy) in streams of flattery
vizards: masks
full of scorpions: (biblical reference – *Revelations 9*)
in them...eterne: they are not immortal
copy: copyright
eterne: eternal, everlasting
There's: there is in that
are assailable: can be overcome
jocund: joyful (see line 28)
cloistered: among cloisters/dim, dark
black Hecate: (last time she was '*pale*', associated with death; now the connection is with the darkness of evil)
shard-borne: flying on scaly wings
yawning peal: curfew
note: notoriety; it will be famous for something evil
chuck: chick (a term of affection)
seeling: blinding (a hawk's eyes would be sewn together, or '*seeled*', until it was trained to wear a hood)
Scarf up: blindfold
tender: merciful
great bond: the lease of life of Banquo and Fleance

Whom we, to gain our peace, have sent to
    peace,   20
Than on the torture of the mind to lie
In restless ecstasy. Duncan is in his grave,
After life's fitful fever he sleeps well,
Treason has done his worst: nor steel, nor poison,
Malice domestic, foreign levy, nothing,
Can touch him further.

L. MACBETH   Come on.
Gentle my lord, sleek o'er your rugged looks,
Be bright and jovial among your guests tonight.

MACBETH   So shall I, love, and so I pray be you.
Let your remembrance apply to Banquo,   ·30
Present him eminence both with eye and tongue –
Unsafe the while that we
Must lave our honours in these flattering streams,
And make our faces vizards to our hearts,
Disguising what they are.

L. MACBETH   You must leave this.

MACBETH   O full of scorpions is my mind, dear wife.
Thou know'st that Banquo, and his Fleance, lives.

L. MACBETH   But in them nature's copy's not eterne.

MACBETH   There's comfort yet, they are assailable;
Then be thou jocund. Ere the bat hath flown   40
His cloistered flight, ere to black Hecate's summons
The shard-borne beetle with his drowsy hums
Hath rung night's yawning peal, there shall be done
A deed of dreadful note.

L. MACBETH   What's to be done?

MACBETH   Be innocent of the knowledge, dearest chuck,
Till thou applaud the deed. Come seeling night,
Scarf up thy tender eye of pitiful day,
And with thy bloody and invisible hand
Cancel and tear to pieces that great bond

Macbeth is in confident mood.

the crow...wood: the rook returns to the rookery
Good things...by ill: (two couplets mark the end of this scene
    and an introduction to the next)

CTIVITIES

Keeping track

Scene 1

1 Why does Macbeth make a fuss of Banquo?
2 Why is Macbeth afraid of Banquo?
3 What does Macbeth intend should happen to Banquo?
4 What does Macbeth tell his visitors in order to persuade them
   to carry out his plan?

Scene 2

5 How does Lady Macbeth deal with Macbeth's mood of
   depression?
6 According to Macbeth, Duncan is better off than he is. Why?

Discussion

1 Why do you think Macbeth does not tell his wife of his plans
   for Banquo?
2 '*Thou marvell'st at my words*' (scene 2 line 54)
   Why should Lady Macbeth be stirred by what her husband is
   saying? How does she react? Is she: shocked, disgusted,
   admiring, proud? What is the reason for her reaction?

Which keeps me pale. Light thickens, and
    the crow   50
Makes wing to th' rooky wood.
Good things of day begin to droop and drowse,
Whiles night's black agents to their preys do rouse.
Thou marvell'st at my words; but hold thee still,
Things bad begun make strong themselves by ill.
So prithee go with me.   [*Exeunt*

Drama

Macbeth and his queen are very concerned to make their first
public entrance as impressive as possible. Imagine that you have
been employed to make sure that this happens. Some of you
could concern yourselves with establishing the correct order for
people to come in. Others need to worry about the clothes that
people should wear.

How would this be different if the play were to be set in
different historical times such as:
- Eleventh-century Scotland
- early seventeenth century when the play was first performed
- late nineteenth-century Wild West of America
- 1920s Chicago with gangsters
- present-day world of big business and takeovers?

Do this as a class, or smaller groups could do different periods.

Character

1 What aspects of Macbeth's character are revealed by:
   - Scene 1 lines 75–91
   - Scene 1 lines 104–108
   - '*Your spirits shine through you.*' (scene 1 line 128) ?
2 In lines 19–22 of scene 2, Macbeth expresses similar thoughts
   to those of Lady Macbeth in lines 4–7 of the same scene. But
   she does not agree with him! On the contrary, she tells him to
   pull himself together.

Does this tell us anything about:
- Lady Macbeth's own character
- how well she knows her husband's character?

3 Bring your CHARACTER LOGS up to date.

Close study

1 Although Banquo has little to say, and indeed he is not seen
   after line 40, scene 1 is all about him. Lines 73–142 concern
   Macbeth's arrangements with the murderers for the killing of
   Banquo, but can you explain how these sections of the scene
   are connected with him?
   lines: 1–10; 11–18; 19–40; 41–48; 48–72

2 A play is written to be performed, not read. In the theatre, an
   audience cannot turn back to previous scenes to remind
   themselves of what has happened. For this reason the
   playwright sometimes has to help the audience to remember
   important pieces of action – or parts of the plot – which relate
   to what is going to happen next. Look again at scene 1 lines
   48–72.
   - Of what important incident is the audience reminded?
   - In which lines of the speech does this reminder occur?
   - Can you think of another effect which this reminder might
     have on the audience? What might they be thinking as they
     listen to these lines?

Writing

Macbeth hints at the backgrounds and histories of the two
murderers. You are going to build up police dossiers on these
two villains. Each will contain:
- background, suggesting reasons for the villainy
- a list of crimes and convictions
- psychologist's report and assessment of intelligence
- army service and record
- documents such as newspaper cuttings and letters
- 'photograph' or identikit picture.
Add any other information you think suitable.

You could be responsible for producing both dossiers, one dossier, or a single item for one of the dossiers. If the whole class worked on the dossiers together then they could be produced very quickly. You could then decide which pieces of the dossiers were 'authentic' and which had to be re-drafted to make them more realistic.

Quiz

Who said the following, and to whom?

1 '*Now if you have a station in the file,*
   Not i' th' worst rank of manhood, say't'

2 '*Things without all remedy*
   Should be without regard: what's done is done'

3 '*Be innocent of the knowledge, dearest chuck,*
   Till thou applaud the deed'

Who said the following, and about whom?

4 '*I fear*
   Thou play'dst most foully for't'

5 '*are bestowed*
   In England and in Ireland, not confessing
   Their cruel parricide'

6 '*And to that dauntless temper of his mind,*
   He hath a wisdom that doth guide his valour'

Who said the following, when, and about what?

7 '*To be thus is nothing,*
   But to be safely thus'

8 '*For Banquo's issue have I filed my mind,*
   For them the gracious Duncan have I murdered'

9 '*Nought's had, all's spent,*
   Where our desire is got without content'

10 '*Things bad begun make strong themselves by ill*'

The murderers await Banquo's return to the palace.

He needs...just: we can trust him because he has told us our
  duties exactly as Macbeth directed
lated: delayed
apace: quickly
timely inn: inn in time
and near...watch: the ones we have been waiting for are
  coming
That are...expectation: who are expected at the banquet
His horses go about: the horses are being taken round to the
  stables
Stand to't: get ready to do it
Let it come down: deliver the rain of blows (following '*rain*',
  line 16)

Scene 3

A park near the palace

Enter three MURDERERS

1ST M.	But who did bid thee join with us?
3RD M.	Macbeth.
2ND M.	He needs not our mistrust, since he delivers Our offices, and what we have to do, To the direction just.
1ST M.	Then stand with us. The west yet glimmers with some streaks of day. Now spurs the lated traveller apace To gain the timely inn, and near approaches The subject of our watch.
3RD M.	Hark! I hear horses.
BANQUO	[*Within*] Give us a light there, ho!
2ND M.	Then 'tis he. The rest That are within the note of expectation 10 Already are i' th' Court.
1ST M.	His horses go about.
3RD M.	Almost a mile; but he does usually, So all men do, from hence to th' palace gate Make it their walk.

Enter BANQUO, *and* FLEANCE *with a torch*

2ND M.	A light, a light!
3RD M.	'Tis he.
1ST M.	Stand to 't.
BANQUO	It will be rain tonight.
1ST M.	Let it come down. [*They assault* BANQUO

Banquo is murdered. In the confusion Fleance escapes.

We have...affair: we have failed to carry out a good part of our commission

Macbeth and Lady Macbeth welcome guests to the banquet. The First Murderer reports to Macbeth the death of Banquo.

degrees: ranks, titles (and therefore places at the table)
At first And last: from beginning to end
society: the guests
keeps her state: remains in her chair of state, throne
we will...welcome: we (i.e. I) will ask her to welcome you
Pronounce it: announce the welcome
my heart speaks: from my heart
encounter: respond to
Be large in mirth: enjoy yourselves freely
'Tis better...within: it is better on the outside of you than inside him

BANQUO	O treachery! Fly good Fleance, fly, fly, fly!
	Thou mayst revenge. O slave! [*Dies.* FLEANCE *escapes*
3RD M.	Who did strike out the light?
1ST M.	Was't not the way?
3RD M.	There's but one down; the son is fled.
2ND M.	We have lost 20
	Best half of our affair.
1ST M.	Well let's away, and say how much is done.

[*Exeunt*

Scene  4

The palace

A banquet prepared. Enter MACBETH, LADY
MACBETH, ROSS, LENNOX, LORDS, *and* ATTENDANTS

MACBETH	You know your own degrees, sit down. At first
	And last the hearty welcome.
LORDS	Thanks to your Majesty.
MACBETH	Ourself will mingle with society,
	And play the humble host.
	Our hostess keeps her state, but in best time
	We will require her welcome.
L. MACBETH	Pronounce it for me, sir, to all our friends,
	For my heart speaks they are welcome.

Enter first MURDERER *to the door*

MACBETH	See, they encounter thee with their hearts' thanks.
	Both sides are even, here I'll sit i' th' midst. 10
	Be large in mirth, anon we'll drink a measure
	The table round. [*Goes to the door*] There's blood
	upon thy face.
1ST M.	'Tis Banquo's then.
MACBETH	'Tis better thee without than he within.

Macbeth is displeased at the news of Fleance's escape. The murderer leaves and Macbeth turns his attention back to the banquet.

dispatched: (see Act 1 scene 5 line 68)
nonpareil: best of all, without equal
fit: mood/fit of terror
perfect: in perfect health
Whole/founded: sound, solid
As broad...air: as free and unrestrained as the surrounding air
cribbed: shut in a small space (similarly '*cabined*', '*confined*', '*bound in*')
saucy: insolent
bides: rests
trenched: deep-cut
The least...nature: any one of which would have killed him
worm: small serpent
Hath nature...breed: in the future he will be a threat
ourselves: each other
the cheer: encouragement which a host should give
The feast...welcome: a feast is no better than a meal which is paid for unless the host keeps repeating, during the festivities, that his guests are welcome
To feed...home: if people only want to eat they can stay at home
From thence...without it: when away from home, the sociability of the host adds, like sauce, to the meal; a gathering of people would be sadly lacking without it
meat/meeting: (play on words)
Now good...appetite: forget about indigestion – eat your fill
health on both: (Macbeth proposes a toast)
our...roofed: the chief nobles of Scotland under one roof
Were: if...were
graced: gracious

	Is he dispatched?
1ST M.	My lord, his throat is cut; that I did for him.
MACBETH	Thou art the best o' th' cut-throats, yet he's good That did the like for Fleance. If thou didst it, Thou art the nonpareil.
1ST M.	Most royal sir, Fleance is 'scaped. 20
MACBETH	Then comes my fit again. I had else been perfect. Whole as the marble, founded as the rock, As broad and general as the casing air; But now I am cabined, cribbed, confined, bound in To saucy doubts and fears. But Banquo's safe?
1ST M.	Ay, my good lord: safe in a ditch he bides, With twenty trenched gashes on his head, The least a death to nature.
MACBETH	Thanks for that. There the grown serpent lies; the worm that's fled Hath nature that in time will venom breed, 30 No teeth for th' present. Get thee gone, tomorrow We'll hear ourselves again. [*Exit* MURDERER
L. MACBETH	My royal lord, You do not give the cheer. The feast is sold That is not often vouched, while 'tis a-making, 'Tis given with welcome. To feed were best at home; From thence the sauce to meat is ceremony, Meeting were bare without it.
MACBETH	Sweet remembrancer! Now, good digestion wait on appetite, And health on both.
LENNOX	May't please your Highness sit. [*The* GHOST OF BANQUO *enters, and sits in* MACBETH'S *seat.*
MACBETH	Here had we now our country's honour roofed, 40 Were the graced person of our Banquo present;

Macbeth intends to sit down but sees Banquo's ghost in
his seat. Macbeth's reaction to the ghost startles the
guests, and Lady Macbeth makes excuses for her husband.
She draws him aside and is scornful of his behaviour.

Who may...mischance: I prefer to regard it as bad-mannered
rather than put it down to bad luck (i.e. he should have
made sure he would be here)

The table's full: (Macbeth glances at the table, looking at no
particular seat)

Here...your Highness?: (Lennox points to the chair on which
Banquo's ghost is sitting. He sees from Macbeth's reaction
that something is wrong.)

Which of...this?:

1 Which of you is playing this trick on me?

2 Which of you killed Banquo? (Macbeth addresses the guests,
assuming that they, too, can see the ghost. If he means **2**
then he is thinking very quickly.)

never shake...me: (the ghost is nodding his head)

The fit is momentary: this condition is short-lived

upon a thought: in a moment

offend: annoy

extend his passion: prolong his agitation

O proper stuff!: what nonsense!

painting: visible representation (not reality)

air-drawn: pictured in the air/drawn through the air

flaws: outbursts of feeling

to: compared to

A woman's story: an old wives' tale

Authorized...grandam: the story-teller says her grandmother
can vouch for the truth of it!

Shame itself: You are shame in person!

	Who may I rather challenge for unkindness,
	Than pity for mischance.
ROSS	His absence, sir,
	Lays blame upon his promise. Please't your Highness
	To grace us with your royal company.
MACBETH	The table's full.
LENNOX	Here is a place reserved, sir.
MACBETH	Where?
LENNOX	Here my good lord. What is't that moves your Highness?
MACBETH	Which of you have done this?
LORDS	What, my good lord?
MACBETH	Thou canst not say I did it; never shake

ROSS His absence, sir,
Lays blame upon his promise. Please't your
Highness
To grace us with your royal company.

MACBETH The table's full.

LENNOX Here is a place reserved, sir.

MACBETH Where?

LENNOX Here my good lord. What is't that moves your
Highness?

MACBETH Which of you have done this?

LORDS What, my good lord?

MACBETH Thou canst not say I did it; never shake   50
Thy gory locks at me.

ROSS Gentlemen rise, his Highness is not well.

L. MACBETH Sit, worthy friends. My lord is often thus,
And hath been from his youth. Pray you keep seat,
The fit is momentary, upon a thought
He will again be well. If much you note him,
You shall offend him, and extend his passion.
Feed, and regard him not. – Are you a man?

MACBETH Ay, and a bold one, that dare look on that
Which might appal the devil.

L. MACBETH O proper stuff!   60
This is the very painting of your fear.
This is the air-drawn dagger which you said
Led you to Duncan. O these flaws and starts,
Impostors to true fear, would well become
A woman's story at a winter's fire,
Authorized by her grandam. Shame itself,
Why do you make such faces? When all's done,
You look but on a stool.

MACBETH Prithee see there. Behold, look, lo, how say you?

When the ghost leaves, Macbeth rejoins his guests, but it reappears and Macbeth's 'fit' returns.

charnel-houses: vaults, tombs
kites: birds of prey which also feed on carrion, dead flesh
our monuments...kites: the stomachs ('*maws*') of kites will be our only memorials (i.e. if corpses will not stay buried then we had better just feed them to kites)
unmanned: without the qualities of manliness
folly: madness
weal: welfare (of a country, usually), general good
Ere humane...weal: before merciful law cleansed society and made it peaceful
The time...That: in the olden days
mortal murders: fatal wounds
muse: be amazed
all to all: all good wishes to everyone
duties/pledge: loyalty, toast (a formal response)
speculation: power of sight

Why what care I? If thou canst nod, speak too. 70
If charnel-houses and our graves must send
Those that we bury back, our monuments
Shall be the maws of kites.   [GHOST *disappears*

L. MACBETH   What, quite unmanned in folly?

MACBETH   If I stand here, I saw him.

L. MACBETH   Fie for shame!

MACBETH   Blood hath been shed ere now, i' th' olden time,
Ere human statute purged the gentle weal;
Ay, and since too, murders have been performed
Too terrible for the ear. The time has been,
That when the brains were out, the man would die,
And there an end. But now they rise again.   80
With twenty mortal murders on their crowns,
And push us from our stools. This is more strange
Than such a murder is.

L. MACBETH   My worthy lord,
Your noble friends do lack you.

MACBETH   I do forget.
Do not muse at me, my most worthy friends,
I have a strange infirmity, which is nothing
To those that know me. Come, love and health to
    all,
Then I'll sit down. Give me some wine, fill full.
I drink to the general joy o' the whole table,

Enter GHOST

And to our dear friend Banquo, whom we miss;   90
Would he were here. To all, and him, we thirst,
And all to all.

LORDS   Our duties, and the pledge.
MACBETH   Avaunt, and quit my sight, let the earth hide thee!
Thy bones are marrowless, thy blood is cold;
Thou hast no speculation in those eyes
Which thou dost glare with!

Lady Macbeth again makes excuses for Macbeth's
behaviour. The ghost leaves again and Macbeth is
prepared to continue with the banquet, but Lady Macbeth
urges the guests to leave. She fears Macbeth will say too
much.

like: in the form of
armed: horned
Hyrcan: (Hyrcania was a region of eastern Europe)
dare me...sword: challenge me in a fight to the death
If trembling...then: if you find fear in me then
protest: proclaim
baby of a girl: baby girl/the puny child of a young mother
Unreal mockery: (Macbeth seems to realize that the ghost is a
    figment of his imagination – for the moment, at least)
Why, so...still: (he composes himself and then turns to his
    guests)
admired disorder: amazing lack of self-control
overcome: pass over/threaten
owe: possess
You make...owe: you make me realize I do not know my own
    nature
mine: the natural ruby of my cheeks
blanched: whitened
At once: to all of you
Stand not...going: (at formal occasions there was an accepted
    order in which the guests would leave – the least important
    first – but Lady Macbeth ushers them all out together)
It will have blood: 'It' refers to Banquo's murder
blood will have blood: (biblical reference – 'Who so sheddeth
    man's blood, by man shall his blood be shed' *Genesis 9, 6*)
Stones: (under which a murdered man has been buried)
trees to speak: (there are various stories in classical legend of
    trees 'speaking')

L. MACBETH   Think of this, good peers,
            But as a thing of custom. 'Tis no other,
            Only it spoils the pleasure of the time.

MACBETH   What man dare, I dare.
            Approach thou like the rugged Russian bear,   100
            The armed rhinoceros, or the Hyrcan tiger;
            Take any shape but that, and my firm nerves
            Shall never tremble. Or be alive again,
            And dare me to the desert with thy sword:
            If trembling I inhabit then, protest me
            The baby of a girl. Hence, horrible shadow,
            Unreal mockery, hence!   [GHOST *disappears*
                            Why, so; being gone,
            I am a man again. Pray you, sit still.

L. MACBETH You have displaced the mirth, broke the good
                meeting.
            With most admired disorder.

MACBETH   Can such things be,   110
            And overcome us like a summer's cloud,
            Without our special wonder? You make me strange
            Even to the disposition that I owe,
            When now I think you can behold such sights,
            And keep the natural ruby of your cheeks,
            When mine is blanched with fear.

ROSS   What sights, my lord?

L. MACBETH I pray you speak not; he grows worse and worse.
            Question enrages him. At once, good night.
            Stand not upon the order of your going.
            But go at once.

LENNOX   Good night, and better health   120
            Attend his Majesty.

L. MACBETH   A kind good night to all.
                [*Exeunt all but* MACBETH *and* LADY MACBETH

MACBETH   It will have blood, they say; blood will have blood.
            Stones have been known to move, and trees
                to speak.

The strain of the evening's events tells on Lady Macbeth. She is quiet. Macbeth intends to learn his future from the witches. He means to continue his bloody course.

Augurs: auguries (telling the future from bird behaviour)
understood relations: connections between things have been understood (when the birds have been correctly interpreted)
maggot-pies: magpies
choughs: jackdaws and similar birds
brought forth...blood: revealed the most secret murderer
the night: the time of night
How say'st...bidding: what do you think of Macduff's refusal to come?
by the way: casually
fee'd: in my pay
betimes: quickly
bent...worst: determined to learn the worst news by the worst means (from the witches)
causes: considerations
I am...o'er: I am so far advanced on this murderous course of action that (like wading across a river of blood) it is as easy to go on as it is to go back
will to hand: must be done
scanned: revealed, come to light
season of all natures: power which preserves all life
strange and self-abuse: strange self-deception
Is the...use: is the beginner's fear which lacks the toughness of experience

It is generally thought that this scene was not written by Shakespeare: the rhythm – and rhyme – differ from other 'witch' scenes.
Hecate is angry with the witches.

---

1 The first witch says Hecate looks angry.

2 Hecate addresses the witches as hags. She is annoyed that the witches spoke to Macbeth without consulting her.

Augurs and understood relations have
By maggot-pies and choughs and rooks brought
   forth
The secret'st man of blood. What is the night?

L. MACBETH   Almost at odds with morning, which is which.

MACBETH   How say'st thou, that Macduff denies his person
At our great bidding?

L. MACBETH   Did you send to him, sir?

MACBETH   I hear it by the way; but I will send.   130
There's not one of them but in his house
I keep a servant fee'd. I will tomorrow,
And betimes I will, to the Weird Sisters.
More shall they speak; for now I am bent
   to know
By the worst means, the worst, for mine own good.
All causes shall give way. I am in blood
Stepped in so far, that should I wade no more,
Returning were as tedious as go o'er.
Strange things I have in head, that will to hand;
Which must be acted ere they may be scanned.   140

L. MACBETH   You lack the season of all natures, sleep.

MACBETH   Come, we'll to sleep. My strange and self-abuse
Is the initiate fear, that wants hard use.
We are yet but young in deed.   [*Exeunt*

Scene 5

The heath

Thunder. Enter the three WITCHES *meeting* HECATE

1ST WITCH   Why how now Hecate, you look angerly.

HECATE   Have I not reason, beldams as you are,
Saucy and overbold? How did you dare

Hecate continues to show her annoyance and tells the witches to prepare for Macbeth's next visit.

2 (contd) She says that she has every right to be angry because they dealt with Macbeth on their own, ignoring her.

3 What is worse, Macbeth is not committed to witchcraft, but merely interested for what he can get out of it.

⟨3⟩

4 She tells them to go back to the Pit of Acheron (their cavern – 'Acheron' was the name of a river of hell) because Macbeth means to visit them again next day. They have to prepare the cauldrons and the spells whilst she takes to the air to catch a drop of magic vapour which is hanging on the moon.

⟨4⟩

5 The vapour will be used to conjure up illusions (apparitions) which will make Macbeth over-confident and lead him to his ruin.

⟨5⟩

6 Hecate leaves and the witches hurry to get things ready before she returns.

⟨6⟩

To trade and traffic with Macbeth
In riddles and affairs of death;
And I, the mistress of your charms,
The close contriver of all harms,
Was never called to bear my part,
Or show the glory of our art?
And, which is worse, all you have done   10
Hath been for a wayward son,
Spiteful, and wrateful, who, as others do,
Loves for his own ends, not for you.
But make amends now: get you gone,
And at the pit of Acheron
Meet me i' th' morning; thither he
Will come to know his destiny.
Your vessels and your spells provide
Your charms, and every thing beside.
I am for the air; this night I'll spend   20
Unto a dismal and a fatal end.
Great business must be wrought ere noon:
Upon the corner of the moon
There hangs a vap'rous drop profound,
I'll catch it ere it come to ground;
And that distilled by magic sleights,
Shall raise such artificial sprites,
As by the strength of their illusion,
Shall draw him on to his confusion.
He shall spurn fate, scorn death, and bear   30
His hopes 'bove wisdom, grace, and fear;
And you all know security
Is mortals' chiefest enemy.
[*Music and a song within*, '*Come away, come
     away,*' *etc.*
Hark! I am call'd; my little spirit, see,
Sits in a foggy cloud, and stays for me.   [*Exit*

1ST WITCH   Come, let's make haste, she'll soon be back again.
                                                  [*Exeunt*

With heavy irony, Lennox recalls recent events and
Macbeth's reactions to them. The lord says that Malcolm
has been welcomed at the English court.

My former...further: you can draw your own conclusions
   from what I have already told you
Only I say: I am just saying that
borne: managed
gracious Duncan...dead: (Macbeth's pity came after Duncan's
   death)
Fleance fled: (Duncan's sons were blamed for his murder
   because they ran away; why not blame Fleance for Banquo's
   murder, then?)
Who cannot...thought: Who can fail to think?
monstrous: unnatural
fact: deed
straight: right away
pious: righteous (loyal to the '*gracious Duncan*')
delinquents: those who abused their duty
thralls: captives
He has...well: he has managed things well for himself/he has
   taken these shocks well
and't: if it
What 'twere: what it means
peace: enough of that
broad: outspoken
failed His presence: did not turn up
tyrant: dictator (Lennox has spoken with heavy irony
   previously: '*How it did grieve Macbeth!*'; '*Was not that nobly
   done?*'; '*He has borne all things well*'. By using the word
   '*tyrant*' he now makes his feelings clear.)
he bestows himself: he has gone
tyrant: (the lord shares Lennox's feelings)
holds the due of birth: withholds his birthright (the crown)

Scene 6

Another castle in Scotland

Enter LENNOX *and another* LORD

LENNOX   My former speeches have but hit your thoughts
         Which can interpret further. Only I say
         Things have been strangely borne. The gracious
              Duncan
         Was pitied of Macbeth – marry he was dead.
         And the right-valiant Banquo walked too late.
         Whom you may say, if 't please you, Fleance killed,
         For Fleance fled – men must not walk too late.
         Who cannot want the thought, how monstrous
         It was for Malcolm and for Donalbain
         To kill their gracious father? Damned fact.   10
         How it did grieve Macbeth! Did he not straight
         In pious rage the two delinquents tear,
         That were the slaves of drink, and thralls of sleep?
         Was not that nobly done? Ay, and wisely too;
         For 'twould have angered any heart alive
         To hear the men deny't. So that I say
         He has borne all things well; and I do think
         That had he Duncan's sons under his key –
         As, and't please heaven, he shall not – they should
              find
         What 'twere to kill a father. So should Fleance.   20
         But peace – for from broad words, and 'cause he
              failed
         His presence at the tyrant's feast, I hear
         Macduff lives in disgrace. Sir, can you tell
         Where he bestows himself?

LORD   The son of Duncan,
         From whom this tyrant holds the due of birth,
         Lives in the English Court, and is received

The lord tells Lennox that Macduff has also gone to the
English court to urge the king to provide an army so that
Macbeth can be defeated and peace be returned to
Scotland.

most pious Edward: Edward the Confessor, King of England
That the...respect: Malcolm is still held in high regard, despite
   his misfortunes
Thither: there
pray: beg
holy King: (according to some of his subjects, Edward the
   Confessor spent too much time in prayer, trying to save his
   soul, when he should have been running the country. He
   was known to these people as Holy Ned.)
upon his aid: on his behalf
wake: call to arms
with Him...work: with God's help
Give to...now: we want to eat and sleep without fear, feast
   without the threat of murder, be loyal to the rightful king
   and know that there are no strings attached to any gift or
   honour we receive; we lack all this at the moment
exasperate the King: annoyed Macbeth
Sent he: Did he send a message?
with an...I': (being met with an utter refusal)
cloudy: sullen
hums: mutters
as who should: as if to
rue: regret
clogs: burdens
to a caution: to be careful
suffering country: (i.e. country suffering)
a hand accursed: (again Lennox's feelings about Mácbeth are
   quite clear)

Of the most pious Edward with such grace,
That the malevolence of fortune nothing
Takes from his high respect. Thither Macduff
Is gone to pray the holy King, upon his aid   30
To wake Northumberland, and warlike Siward,
That by the help of these, with Him above
To ratify the work, we may again
Give to our tables meat, sleep to our nights,
Free from our feasts and banquets bloody knives,
Do faithful homage, and receive free honours,
All which we pine for now. And this report
Hath so exasperate the King, that he
Prepares for some attempt of war.

LENNOX   Sent he to Macduff?

LORD   He did; and with an absolute 'Sir, not I',   40
The cloudy messenger turns me his back,
And hums, as who should say, 'You'll rue the time
That clogs me with this answer.'

LENNOX   And that well might
Advise him to a caution, to hold what distance
His wisdom can provide. Some holy angel
Fly to the Court of England, and unfold
His message ere he come, that a swift blessing
May soon return to this our suffering country
Under a hand accursed.

LORD   I'll send my prayers with him.

                                        [*Exeunt*

ACTIVITIES

Keeping track

Scene 3

1 What is the result of the attempt to murder Banquo and Fleance?

Scene 4

2 Which stranger appears at the banquet with news for Macbeth?
3 What causes Macbeth to react strangely and violently at the banquet?
4 How does Lady Macbeth excuse her husband's behaviour to their guests?
5 What is Lady Macbeth's attitude to Macbeth when she takes him aside?
6 How does Lady Macbeth finally prevent Macbeth from revealing too much to the guests?
7 How does Macbeth know so much about his Thanes?

Scene 5

8 What does Hecate order the witches to do?

Scene 6

9 Where has Macduff gone, and why?
10 How has Macduff offended Macbeth concerning the coronation and the banquet?

Discussion

'The Ghost of Banquo enters'
The ghost enters twice. On each occasion Macbeth is taken by surprise to see him sitting in his place. If you were producing the play, how would you get the ghost on-stage (and off-stage twice)

in the most effective way?
To help you with your decision/s, look at what is being said
before the ghost enters (or leaves).

- In what positions will the actors be? (Whether they are
  standing or sitting might be very important.)
- Where will the audience's attention be? Can you use this
  information to your advantage?

Follow up
See DRAMA 2, below.

Drama

1 In groups of five or six choreograph and then enact the murder
  of Banquo in slow motion. A useful rehearsal technique here is
  to make the sound effects of the fight like those you would
  read in a comic. What kind of weapons would be used?
2 Set up the classroom for the banquet. You need to decide who
  will be there and where they will sit. Using FORUM THEATRE
  (see page 228), explore the First Murderer's appearance (scene
  4 line 8). See whether the ideas you came up with in
  DISCUSSION, above, will actually work in practice.

Character

1 At the end of scene 4 Macbeth seems to be totally recovered
  from his frenzy at seeing the ghost. What is his attitude to:
  - Macduff
  - the witches
  - the future ?
2 At the end of scene 4 Lady Macbeth says very little. She seems
  tired and drained by the events of the evening. Do you think
  that she is suffering from a temporary tiredness, or is there
  more to it? Is the situation of constant deceit and fear of
  discovery becoming just too much for her? Is she beginning to
  lose the strength she showed earlier?
     What do you see happening to her in the future?
3 Bring your CHARACTER LOGS up to date. Close your log on
  Banquo.

Close study

1 Look again at scene 4 lines 46–121. The audience know what is happening because they can see the ghost; and Macbeth knows what is happening.
   - Lady Macbeth thinks she knows what is happening, but does she really?
   - The guests are completely puzzled: what explanation do you think they might have for Macbeth's behaviour? Do they believe Lady Macbeth?

2 At the end of scene 4 lines 128–144:
   a Which lines suggest that Macbeth is already thinking of his next victim?
   b Can you suggest one of the 'strange things' which might be in Macbeth's mind?
   c Which recurring theme of the play is referred to by Lady Macbeth?
   d Which word tells us that Macbeth believes he has imagined Banquo's ghost?
   e The rhyming couplet of lines 139–140 rounds off what Macbeth has just been saying. But:
      - what is the purpose of the second couplet lines 142–143?
      - what is the effect of the last line of the scene, added after the final couplet?

3 a Look at Lennox's speech scene 6 lines 1–20, before he uses the word 'tyrant' to describe Macbeth. Which lines would he speak with irony (see GLOSSARY page 238)?
   b How do we know that the lord has understood Lennox's true feelings about Macbeth?

Writing

1 'His royalty of nature'
Write a paragraph or two about Banquo, describing his admirable qualities: those qualities, indeed, which might have been fitting for a king.

2 **Loyalty his downfall**

Write another paragraph or two explaining why Banquo is
murdered; how he might have survived if he had spoken out;
and how it is ironic that he should be so loyal to Macbeth. Use
quotations to illustrate your main points.

Quiz

Who said the following, and to whom?

1 '*fly, fly, fly!*'
2 '*never shake
    Thy gory locks at me*'
3 '*When all's done,
    You look but on a stool*'

Who said the following, and about whom?

4 '*safe in a ditch he bides,
    With twenty trenched gashes on his head*'
5 '*the worm that's fled
    Hath nature that in time will venom breed*'
6 '*he grows worse and worse.
    Question enrages him*'

Who said the following, when, and about what?

7 '*'Tis better thee without than he within*'
8 '*But now I am cabined, cribbed, confined, bound in
    To saucy doubts and fears*'
9 '*O proper stuff!
    This is the very painting of your fear*'
10 '*Avaunt, and quit my sight, let the earth hide thee!*'

The witches prepare the cauldron whilst they await Macbeth's arrival.

brinded: brindled, streaked
hedge-pig: hedgehog
Harpier: a familiar spirit (which gives the signal to start)
Sweltered...got: has sweated poison (for a month) and been captured in its sleep
Double: increase twofold (also suggests deception – double meaning)
Fillet...snake: slice of a snake from the fens
fork: forked tongue
blind-worm: slow-worm (once believed to be poisonous)
howlet: owlet
Witch's mummy: medicine prepared from a witch's corpse
maw and gulf: stomach and gut
ravined: gorged, glutted
digged i' th' dark: dug up at night (for full poisonous effect)

Act four

Scene 1

The 'Pit of Acheron'

Thunder. Enter the three WITCHES

1ST WITCH	Thrice the brinded cat hath mewed.
2ND WITCH	Thrice and once the hedge-pig whined
3RD WITCH	Harpier cries ''Tis time, 'Tis time.'
1ST WITCH	Round about the cauldron go;
	In the poisoned entrails throw.
	Toad, that under cold stone
	Days and nights hast thirty-one
	Sweltered venom sleeping got,
	Boil thou first i' th' charmed pot.
ALL	Double, double toil and trouble;
	Fire burn, and cauldron bubble.
2ND WITCH	Fillet of a fenny snake,
	In the cauldron boil and bake;
	Eye of newt, and toe of frog,
	Wool of bat, and tongue of dog,
	Adder's fork, and blind-worm's sting,
	Lizard's leg, and howlet's wing,
	For a charm of powerful trouble,
	Like a hell-broth boil and bubble.
ALL	Double, double toil and trouble;
	Fire burn, and cauldron bubble.
3RD WITCH	Scale of dragon, tooth of wolf,
	Witches' mummy, maw and gulf
	Of the ravined salt-sea shark,
	Root of hemlock digged i' th' dark,
	Liver of blaspheming Jew,

10

20

Hecate comes to check that all is ready. The witches dance to seal the charm. Hecate leaves and Macbeth arrives, commanding the witches to tell him what he wants to know.

---

slips of yew: cuttings of yew (a graveyard tree, thought to be poisonous)

Slivered: sliced off

moon's eclipse: a time of ill-omen

Turk/Tartar: in Shakespeare's time, people noted for their cruelty

birth-strangled: strangled at birth (and so unbaptized)

Ditch-delivered...drab: born in a ditch of a prostitute

slab: stodgy

chaudron: guts

ingredience: ingredients

Enter HECATE *and the three other* WITCHES: (The stage directions and the following five lines are almost certainly not by Shakespeare. The extra witches help with the song and dance.)

By the...thumbs: pricking thumbs (pins and needles) was an omen of evil

locks/knocks: (the cavern would be protected by a charm not a locked door)

secret: unknown

black...hags: those who practise black magic

without a name: nameless, too horrible to give a name

conjure: call on

that which you profess: witchcraft

Though you...sicken: (Macbeth is prepared to sacrifice the natural world to get what he wants – see Act 3 scene 2 line 16)

yesty: frothing

Confound: wreck

navigation: shipping

	Gall of goat, and slips of yew
	Slivered in the moon's eclipse,
	Nose of Turk, and Tartar's lips,
	Finger of birth-strangled babe 30
	Ditch-delivered by a drab,
	Make the gruel thick and slab.
	Add thereto a tiger's chaudron,
	For th' ingredients of our cauldron.
ALL	Double, double toil and trouble;
	Fire burn, and cauldron bubble.
2ND WITCH	Cool it with a baboon's blood,
	Then the charm is firm and good.

Enter HECATE *and the three other* WITCHES

HECATE	O well done! I commend your pains,
	And every one shall share i' th' gains. 40
	And now about the cauldron sing,
	Live elves and fairies in a ring,
	Enchanting all that you put in.

[*Music and song, 'Black spirits', etc.*

[*Exit* HECATE

2ND WITCH	By the pricking of my thumbs,
	Something wicked this way comes:
	Open, locks,
	Whoever knocks.

Enter MACBETH

MACBETH	How now, you secret, black, and midnight hags!
	What is't you do?
ALL	A deed without a name.
MACBETH	I conjure you, by that which you profess, 50
	Howe'er you come to know it, answer me.
	Though you untie the winds and let them fight
	Against the churches; though the yesty waves
	Confound and swallow navigation up;

The First Apparition appears from the cauldron. It is a helmeted head, and it warns Macbeth to be cautious of Macduff.

---

bladed corn be lodged: unripe corn be blown flat
slope: bend down
treasure...together: precious seeds from which come all living things are thrown into disorder
till destruction sicken: until destruction is sick of destroying
our masters: (the evil spirits whom the witches serve, and who will take the form of apparitions)
nine: (mystic number)
farrow: piglets
sweaten: sweated
gibbet: scaffold
armed head: a head wearing a helmet
He knows thy thought: (the head could be a representation of Macbeth's head, in which case this line is ironic)
Macbeth! Macbeth! Macbeth!: (Is it significant that this is said three times?)
harped: touched on

Though bladed corn be lodged, and trees blown
    down;
Though castles topple on their warders' heads;
Though palaces and pyramids do slope
Their heads to their foundations; though the
    treasure
Of nature's germens tumble all together,
Even till destruction sicken; answer me   60
To what I ask you.

1ST WITCH   Speak.

2ND WITCH   Demand.

3RD WITCH   We'll answer.

1ST WITCH   Say if thou'dst rather hear it from our mouths,
Or from our masters?

MACBETH   Call 'em, let me see 'em.

1ST WITCH   Pour in sow's blood, that hath eaten
Her nine farrow; grease that's sweaten
From the murderer's gibbet, throw
Into the flame.

ALL   Come high or low;
Thyself and office deftly show.

Thunder. 1ST APPARITION, *an armed head*

MACBETH   Tell me, thou unknown power –

1ST WITCH   He knows thy thought.
Hear his speech, but say thou nought.   70

1ST APP.   Macbeth, Macbeth, Macbeth, beware Macduff;
Beware the Thane of Fife. Dismiss me. Enough.
                             [*Descends*

MACBETH   Whate'er thou art, for thy good caution thanks;
Thou hast harped my fear aright. But one word
    more –

1ST WITCH   He will not be commanded. Here's another,
More potent than the first.

The Second Apparition tells Macbeth that no man born of woman can harm him. The Third Apparition says that he will not be beaten until Birnham Wood moves to Dunsinane. Macbeth is filled with confidence.

bloody child: child covered in blood

yet I'll...sure: I have been assured of the future but I'll make doubly certain

take a bond of fate: compel fate to fulfil its promise

That I may...thunder: so that I can prove my cowardly fears to be groundless, and I shall be able to sleep, even through thunder

issue: child

round And top: crown and highest symbol

lion-mettled: lion-spirited

chafes: rages

impress: enlist

bodements: prophecies

live the...nature: live out his natural life

mortal custom: natural death

issue: descendants

this kingdom: (the prophecy did not specify where Banquo's descendants would reign, and Macbeth pins his hopes on this question)

Thunder. 2ND APPARITION, *a bloody child*

2ND APP.   Macbeth, Macbeth, Macbeth!

MACBETH   Had I three ears, I'd hear thee.

2ND APP.   Be bloody, bold and resolute; laugh to scorn
             The power of man, for none of woman born   80
             Shall harm Macbeth.   [*Descends*

MACBETH   Then live Macduff, what need I fear of thee?
            But yet I'll make assurance double sure,
            And take a bond of fate. Thou shalt not live;
            That I may tell pale-hearted fear it lies,
            And sleep in spite of thunder.

            Thunder. 3RD APPARITION, *a child crowned, with a
               tree in his hand*

                                     What is this,
            That rises like the issue of a king,
            And wears upon his baby brow the round
            And top of sovereignty?

ALL   Listen, but speak not to't.

3RD APP.   Be lion-mettled, proud and take no care   90
             Who chafes, who frets, or where conspirers are.
             Macbeth shall never vanquished be, until
             Great Birnam wood to high Dunsinane hill
             Shall come against him.   [*Descends*

MACBETH   That will never be.
            Who can impress the forest, bid the tree
            Unfix his earth-bound root? Sweet bodements,
               good!
            Rebellious dead, rise never till the wood
            Of Birnam rise, and our high-placed Macbeth
            Shall live the lease of nature, pay his breath
            To time and mortal custom. Yet my heart   100
            Throbs to know one thing: tell me, if your art
            Can tell so much, shall Banquo's issue ever
            Reign in this kingdom?

At Macbeth's insistence the witches conjure up a 'show' of
eight kings, indicating that Banquo's descendants will
indeed be crowned. Macbeth is totally dejected.

---

an eternal...you: (this is surely a sign of Macbeth's
desperation!)

noise: music

shadows: images

so: in the same way

A show of eight KINGS: (The 'show' consists of eight Stuart
kings, ancestors of James I. Tactfully, Shakespeare does not
include Mary, Queen of Scots, James's mother. James
succeeded to the throne after her death, which he did little
to prevent.)

sear: burn

Start: jump from your sockets (so that I can see no more)

crack of doom: trumpet blast of Judgement Day

glass: mirror, the glass of which is cut to produce illusions (the
equivalent of a crystal ball)

twofold...sceptres: (the Scottish coronation used one orb and
one sceptre; the English, one orb and two sceptres. This is
another tribute to James, indicating that his descendants
would inherit the throne which he had united.)

blood-boltered: his hair matted with blood

sprites: spirits

antic round: grotesque circular dance

great King: Macbeth/James I

Our duties...pay: we paid our respects to make him welcome

Ay, sir...pay: (this is another section which many regard as
being written by a different author)

ALL	Seek to know no more.
MACBETH	I will be satisfied. Deny me this,
	And an eternal curse fall on you. Let me know.
	Why sinks that cauldron, and what noise is this?

                                                        [Oboes

1ST WITCH	Show!
2ND WITCH	Show!
3RD WITCH	Show!
ALL	Show his eyes, and grieve his heart; 110
	Come like shadows, so depart.

    A show of eight KINGS, *the last with a glass in his*
      hand; BANQUO *following*

MACBETH	Thou art too like the spirit of Banquo. Down!
	Thy crown does sear mine eyeballs; and thy hair,
	Thou other gold-bound brow, is like the first.
	A third is like the former. Filthy hags,
	Why do you show me this? A fourth? Start, eyes!
	What, will the line stretch out to th' crack of doom?
	Another yet? A seventh? I'll see no more.
	And yet the eighth appears, who bears a glass,
	Which shows me many more; and some I see 120
	That twofold balls and treble sceptres carry:
	Horrible sight! Now I see 'tis true,
	For the blood-boltered Banquo smiles upon me,
	And points at them for his. What, is this so?
1ST WITCH	Ay, sir, all this is so. But why
	Stands Macbeth thus amazedly?
	Come sisters, cheer we up his sprites,
	And show the best of our delights.
	I'll charm the air to give a sound,
	While you perform your antic round; 130
	That this great King may kindly say,
	Our duties did his welcome pay.

                            [Music. The WITCHES *dance, and vanish*

Macbeth calls in Lennox, who has not seen the witches but he does have news that Macduff has gone to England. Macbeth intends to seize Macduff's castle and slaughter his family.

pernicious: ruinous

aye: for ever

without there: the person outside

***Enter* LENNOX:** (Despite Lennox's view of Macbeth in Act 3 scene 6, he stays with him. He has been on guard outside the cavern.)

Infected by: infected be

And damned...them: (irony – Macbeth does trust them and he is damned)

Fled to England?: (He sounds surprised, and yet with Macbeth's network of spies, Act 3 scene 6 lines 37–39 seems more likely!)

Time, thou...exploits: my terrible plans have been thwarted by time

The flighty...with it: intentions arrived at quickly will never be carried out unless the action is equally swift

firstlings: first things (plans, actions)

give to...sword: cut down

souls That...line: his family

sights: apparitions

MACBETH   Where are they? Gone? Let this pernicious hour
             Stand aye accursed in the calendar.
             Come in, without there!

             Enter LENNOX

LENNOX   What's your Grace's will?

MACBETH   Saw you the Weird Sisters?

LENNOX   No, my lord.

MACBETH   Came they not by you?

LENNOX   No indeed, my lord.

MACBETH   Infected by the air whereon they ride,
             And damned all those that trust them. I did hear
             The galloping of horse. Who was't came by?   140

LENNOX   'Tis two or three, my lord, that bring you word
             Macduff is fled to England.

MACBETH   Fled to England?

LENNOX   Ay my good lord.

MACBETH   Time, thou anticipat'st my dread exploits.
             The flighty purpose never is o'ertook
             Unless the deed go with it. From this moment
             The very firstlings of my heart shall be
             The firstlings of my hand. And even now,
             To crown my thoughts with acts, be it thought and
                done.
             The castle of Macduff I will surprise,   150
             Seize upon Fife, give to the edge o' th' sword
             His wife, his babes, and all unfortunate souls
             That trace him in his line. No boasting like a fool;
             This deed I'll do before this purpose cool.
             But no more sights! Where are these gentlemen?
             Come bring me where they are.   [*Exeunt*

ACTIVITIES

Keeping track

1 What is the First Apparition and what is its warning?
2 What is the Second Apparition and what is its message?
3 What is the Third Apparition and what is its message?
4 What is the question which Macbeth asks, the answer to which is given by the 'show of kings'?
5 What news does Lennox give Macbeth?
6 What is Macbeth's plan regarding Macduff?

Discussion

1 In the last scene Lennox made clear his feelings about Macbeth, and yet he is still serving him. Why might this be?
2 How is it possible for Macbeth to say '*And damned all those that trust them*' (line 138), when he himself is prepared to believe what the witches have prophesied? Does he accept that he is damned; or does he think perhaps that he has so much power that they cannot touch him? Do you think there are other reasons?
3 Would it be fair to say that Macbeth is a victim in this scene, goaded on to greater evil by the witches' prophecies?
4 We often expect to see some motivation for evil actions, or at least a reason for them, such as some form of gain. Is there any evidence of this with the witches? What do they hope to gain from their tempting of Macbeth?

Drama

1 Work as a whole class. Divide up the lines that the witches speak, up to line 47, but exclude Hecate's lines, 39–43. Everyone says the lines given to ALL, which leave 36 lines to be divided among the class. Learn your lines. Enjoy these words; relish the sounds and rhythms they make. Practise the lines

separately and then bring the whole ritual to life.

2 Carry on with the rest of the scene in the same way, dividing up the lines between you. Either one of you or your teacher could take the part of Macbeth.

3 Imagine you are working for a touring company which is performing Macbeth with a small cast. The director thinks it would be a good idea to use puppets in this scene to represent the apparitions, the line of kings and the ghost of Banquo. You have been asked to produce some designs.

   The director wants them to be particularly horrific and as big as possible. She needs preliminary sketches and ideas quickly. Bring your designs to a production meeting. Be prepared to justify the designs by referring to the text.

4 Suppose Lennox is lying and that he has seen and overheard Macbeth's meeting with the witches. Work in groups of five or six. One person is Lennox and the others his friends, Ross, his wife, or Malcolm's spies. What can he tell? Would his information be valuable?

Character

1 What is Macbeth's attitude to the witches throughout this scene? Can you explain why he is like this towards them?

2 What do lines 144–156, and especially 150–153, tell us about Macbeth's present state of mind?
   How does this relate to Act 3 scene 4 lines 142–143?

3 Bring your CHARACTER LOGS up to date.

Close study

1 What is the dramatic purpose of the witches' detailed charm, lines 1–38 and 64–67? Would the same effect have been achieved if Macbeth had entered at the beginning of the scene, and the audience had been left to assume that the charm was already '*firm and good*'?

2 In this scene, what has made Macbeth feel more secure, and what has made him more desperate?

3 The three major themes of this play (the Supernatural, Evil and

Ambition) are evident in most lines of this scene.
- On a page mark out 156 sections which will represent the 156 lines of the scene. This is best done on A4 graph paper.
- To make the next part of the work easier, number every tenth (or fifth, if you wish) section.
- Read the scene again, and using a different colour for each theme, fill in those sections/lines dealing with the supernatural, evil and ambition. Some lines concern both the supernatural and ambition, or evil and ambition; those sections will contain two colours. There might even be sections with three colours.
- You should finish with a visual representation of the themes of the scene, and be able to say which is the main one.

Follow up
See WRITING 2, below.

Writing

1 Write Macbeth's diary containing his thoughts about, and reactions to, the day's events. You will cover in detail the apparitions, the show of kings and Banquo's ghost, and your (Macbeth's) feelings about them. But you will also need to mention your thoughts about the witches and your plans for the future. A diary can be written in note form: there is no need for full sentences.

2 **The Supernatural, Evil, Ambition**
   a Which of these do you think is the main theme in Act 4 scene 1?
   b Write a short essay about the theme you have chosen:
      - in your first paragraph say very briefly how the supernatural (or evil or ambition) has influenced the action of the play up to the end of Act 3
      - in the body of your essay, in one or two paragraphs, show how Shakespeare deals with the main theme in this scene
      - use two or three quotations to illustrate what you say

- in your conclusion predict what effect this scene will have on the rest of the play (i.e. will the apparitions be any more reliable than the witches?)

Quiz

Who said the following, and to whom?
1 'How now, you secret, black, and midnight hags!'
2 'Macbeth, Macbeth, Macbeth, beware Macduff'
3 'none of woman born
    Shall harm Macbeth'

Who said the following, and about whom?
4 'By the pricking of my thumbs,
    Something wicked this way comes'
5 'But yet I'll make assurance double sure,
    And take a bond of fate'
6 'Infected be the air whereon they ride,
    And damned all those that trust them'

Who said the following, when, and about what?
7 'Double, double toil and trouble;
    Fire burn, and cauldron bubble'
8 'Who can impress the forest, bid the tree
    Unfix his earth-bound root?'
9 'And yet the eighth appears, who bears a glass,
    Which shows me many more'
10 'give to the edge o' th' sword
    His wife, his babes, and all unfortunate souls
    That trace him in his line'

Ross has told Lady Macduff about her husband's flight to
England. Lady Macduff condemns Macduff's selfishness
in running away – as she sees it – at such a dangerous
time.

patience: self-control
When our...traitors: he has not been disloyal to Macbeth, but
his fear has made him a traitor to his family
titles: possessions
wants the natural touch: he lacks nature's instincts
poor: feeble
All is...love: (biblical reference – 'There is no fear in love'
St John 4, 18)
fear: (for himself)
love: (for his family)
coz: cousin (a general name indicating close friendship/
relationship)
school: control
fits o' th' season: conditions of the time
do not know ourselves: (...to be traitors)
when we hold...move: we listen to rumours because we are
afraid, and, although we do not know what we are afraid of,
our minds are in turmoil
Things at...cease: things are not going to get much worse
pretty: fine (Ross is speaking to Macduff's son)

Scene  2

Macduff's castle

Enter LADY MACDUFF, *her* SON, *and* ROSS

L. MACDUFF   What had he done, to make him fly the land?

ROSS   You must have patience, madam.

L. MACDUFF   He had none.
His flight was madness. When our actions do not,
Our fears do make us traitors.

ROSS   You know not
Whether it was his wisdom, or his fear.

L. MACDUFF   Wisdom! to leave his wife, to leave his babes,
His mansion, and his titles in a place
From whence himself does fly? He loves us not;
He wants the natural touch. For the poor wren,
The most diminutive of birds, will fight,   10
Her young ones in her nest, against the owl.
All is the fear, and nothing is the love;
As little is the wisdom, where the flight
So runs against all reason.

ROSS   My dearest coz,
I pray you school yourself. But for your husband,
He is noble, wise, judicious, and best knows
The fits o' th' season. I dare not speak much
      further,
But cruel are the times, when we are traitors,
And do not know ourselves; when we hold rumour
From what we fear, yet know not what we fear,   20
But float upon a wild and violent sea
Each way and move. I take my leave of you.
Shall not be long but I'll be here again.
Things at the worst will cease, or else climb upward
To what they were before. My pretty cousin,

Ross leaves, and Lady Macduff and her son show a shared, loving relationship in their conversation.

It would…discomfort: I would weep and you would be
embarrassed
Sirrah: (used by parents to children, as well as masters to
servants)
dead: (i.e. he might as well be dead; we shall not see him
again)
As birds do: (biblical reference – 'fowls of the air.. your
heavenly father feedeth them' *Matthew 6, 26*)
thou'dst never…gin: you are too innocent to fear bird traps
lime: bird-lime, a sticky substance spread on twigs to catch
birds
pitfall: fowler's snare
gin: trap
Poor birds…set for: traps are not intended to catch wretched
birds
to sell again: (and make a profit)
wit enough for thee: you are bright for your age
Was my…traitor: (he listened earlier, and understood)
swears, and lies: breaks an oath of allegiance/breaks marriage
vows

	Blessing upon you!
L. MACDUFF	Fathered he is, and yet he's fatherless.
ROSS	I am so much a fool, should I stay longer,
	It would be my disgrace and your discomfort.
	I take my leave at once. [*Exit*
L. MACDUFF	Sirrah, your father's dead, 30
	And what will you do now? How will you live?
SON	As birds do, mother.
L. MACDUFF	What, with worms, and flies?
SON	With what I get I mean, and so do they.
L. MACDUFF	Poor bird, thou'dst never fear the net nor lime,
	The pitfall nor the gin.
SON	Why should I, mother? Poor birds they are not set for.
	My father is not dead, for all your saying.
L. MACDUFF	Yes, he is dead. How wilt thou do for a father?
SON	Nay, how will you do for a husband?
L. MACDUFF	Why, I can buy me twenty at any market. 40
SON	Then you'll buy 'em to sell again.
L. MACDUFF	Thou speak'st with all thy wit, and yet i' faith
	With wit enough for thee.
SON	Was my father a traitor, mother?
L. MACDUFF	Ay, that he was.
SON	What is a traitor?
L. MACDUFF	Why one that swears, and lies.
SON	And be all traitors that do so?
L. MACDUFF	Every one that does so is a traitor, and must be hanged.
SON	And must they all be hanged that swear and lie? 50
L. MACDUFF	Every one.
SON	Who must hang them?
L. MACDUFF	Why, the honest men.

A messenger arrives to warn Lady Macduff that danger
threatens. She hesitates for some moments and that is too
long: the murderers enter.

---

enow: enough

Then the liars...them: (a 'clever' conclusion, but ironic in
view of what is to come)

poor: (despite her son's light-heartedness, Lady Macduff's
repetition of '*poor*' when addressing him throughout this
scene shows that she feels they are in a desperate situation)

prattler: one who talks a lot

in your...perfect: I am perfectly aware of your high rank

doubt: fear

nearly: closely

homely: lowly

To do...person: not to warn you would be an act of fiercest
cruelty, and fiercest cruelty is too close to you

laudable: praiseworthy

sometime: sometimes

Accounted...folly: reckoned to be dangerous foolishness

faces: (possibly masks; or they could be hiding their faces)

unsanctified: unholy (the English court was indeed sanctified)

shag-eared: shaggy hair over the ears

SON	Then the liars and swearers are fools; for there are liars and swearers enow to beat the honest men, and hang up them.
L. MACDUFF	Now God help thee, poor monkey. But how wilt thou do for a father?
SON	If he were dead, you'd weep for him; if you would not, it were a good sign that I should 60 quickly have a new father.
L. MACDUFF	Poor prattler, how thou talk'st!

Enter a MESSENGER

MESSENGER	Bless you fair dame. I am not to you known, Though in your state of honour I am perfect. I doubt some danger does approach you nearly. If you will take a homely man's advice, Be not found here; hence with your little ones. To fright you thus, methinks I am too savage; To do worse to you were fell cruelty, Which is too nigh your person. Heaven preserve you, 70 I dare abide no longer. [*Exit*
L. MACDUFF	Whither should I fly? I have done no harm. But I remember now I am in this earthly world, where to do harm Is often laudable, to do good sometime Accounted dangerous folly. Why then, alas, Do I put up that womanly defence, To say I have done no harm?

Enter MURDERERS

What are these faces?

1ST M.	Where is your husband?
L. MACDUFF	I hope in no place so unsanctified Where such as thou mayst find him.
1ST M.	He's a traitor. 80
SON	Thou liest thou shag-eared villain.

Her son is killed, and Lady Macduff runs away,
postponing her own death by only a few moments.

egg: immature weakling
Young fry of treachery: offspring (young fish) of a traitor

Macduff is at the English court seeking Malcolm's help,
but Malcolm is suspicious of him.

bosoms: hearts
fast: tightly
mortal: deadly
Bestride: defend, stand over
our down-fallen birthdom: our native land, which has been
    laid low
Each new morn...cry: (dramatic irony after the previous
    scene)
that it resounds: so that heaven echoes
felt: suffered
Like syllable of dolour: the same cry of misery
wail: mourn for
redress: put right
As: when
to friend: favourable
perchance: perhaps
sole: very
honest: honourable
loved him well: served him loyally
He hath not touched you: he has not done anything to you
young: (and therefore not dangerous)
but something...god: you might have learned something
    about Macbeth from the way he has treated me, and think it
    wise to offer me up as a sort of sacrifice

1ST M.	What, you egg!
	[*Stabs him*

Young fry of treachery!

SON	He has killed me, mother:

Run away, I pray you.   [*Dies*
[*Exit* LADY MACDUFF, *crying* 'Murder!' *and*
                    pursued by the MURDERERS

Scene 3

England: the King's palace

Enter MALCOLM *and* MACDUFF

MALCOLM   Let us seek out some desolate shade, and there
            Weep our sad bosoms empty.

MACDUFF   Let us rather
            Hold fast the mortal sword, and like good men,
            Bestride our down-fallen birthdom. Each new
                morn,
            New widows howl, new orphans cry, new sorrows
            Strike heaven on the face, that it resounds
            As if it felt with Scotland, and yelled out
            Like syllable of dolour.

MALCOLM   What I believe, I'll wail;
            What know, believe; and what I can redress,
            As I shall find the time to friend, I will.   10
            What you have spoke, it may be so perchance.
            This tyrant, whose sole name blisters our tongues,
            Was once thought honest; you have loved him well;
            He hath not touched you yet. I am young, but
                something
            You may discern of him through me, and wisdom
            To offer up a weak, poor, innocent lamb
            T' appease an angry god.

MACDUFF   I am not treacherous.

Macduff is dismayed at Malcolm's attitude to him, and fears for Scotland's future. Malcolm appreciates Macduff's love of his country but warns him that Scotland will be worse off when Macbeth is removed from power.

---

may recoil...charge: might give way if a king commands

But I...pardon: (Malcolm apologizes for hurting Macduff's feelings, but continues to test him)

transpose: change

still: always

brightest: Satan (Satan/Lucifer was the brightest angel in heaven until he rebelled against God and was cast out.)

Though all...so: (evil men might try to deceive by appearing good, but good men also look good:

   1 *'There's no art to find the mind's construction in the face'*

   2 *'look like th' innocent flower, But be the serpent under't'*

   3 *'False face must hide what the false heart doth know'*)

I have lost...doubts: Macduff's hope is gone, but Malcolm says that perhaps his hopes were dashed for the same reason (*'even there'*) that Malcolm is suspicious

Why in...leave-taking?: (this is why Malcolm suspects Macduff, and why Macduff has no hope of proving his sincerity. Malcolm thinks Macduff must be sure of his family's safety and therefore in league with Macbeth.)

rawness: defencelessness

precious motives: dear reasons for being, existing

Let not...safeties: do not let my suspicions discredit you; they are for my self-protection

rightly just: perfectly honourable

basis: foundation

wear thou thy wrongs: be open about your crimes

affeered: confirmed (play on words, *'affeered'/'affeared'*)

to boot: as well, in addition

in my right: to support my rightful claim

gracious England: the King of England, Edward the Confessor

tread upon...head: (a method of killing serpents)

wear it...sword: show off his head on the point of my sword

MALCOLM	But Macbeth is.
	A good and virtuous nature may recoil
	In an imperial charge. But I shall crave your
	pardon. 20
	That which you are, my thoughts cannot transpose:
	Angels are bright still, though the brightest fell.
	Though all things foul would wear the brows of
	grace,
	Yet grace must still look so.
MACDUFF	I have lost my hopes.
MALCOLM	Perchance even there where I did find my doubts.
	Why in this rawness left you wife and child,
	Those precious motives, those strong knots of love,
	Without leave-taking? I pray you,
	Let not my jealousies be your dishonours,
	But mine own safeties. You may be rightly just, 30
	Whatever I shall think.
MACDUFF	Bleed, bleed, poor country;
	Great tyranny, lay thou thy basis sure,
	For goodness dare not check thee; wear thou thy
	wrongs,
	The title is affeered. Fare thee well, lord;
	I would not be the villain that thou think'st
	For the whole space that's in the tyrant's grasp,
	And the rich East to boot.
MALCOLM	Be not offended;
	I speak not as in absolute fear of you.
	I think our country sinks beneath the yoke;
	It weeps, it bleeds, and each new day a gash 40
	Is added to her wounds. I think withal,
	There would be hands uplifted in my right;
	And here from gracious England have I offer
	Of goodly thousands. But, for all this,
	When I shall tread upon the tyrant's head,
	Or wear it on my sword, yet my poor country
	Shall have more vices than it had before,

Malcolm says that when he comes to the throne the people of Scotland will want Macbeth back. When he claims that his lust knows no bounds Macduff is surprised, but assures him that it need be no problem.

sundry: various
By him: through him
What should he be?: Who can you be talking about?
grafted: implanted
opened: revealed ('*opened*' like a bud)
confineless harms: limitless evils
legions: ranks, army
top: surpass
grant him...malicious: admit that he is bloodthirsty, lustful, greedy, dishonourable, lying, violent, evil
smacking: full
voluptuousness: lust
Your: Scotland's
cistern: pit, pool
continent...o'erbear: would overcome all restraining forces
will: lust
Boundless...tyranny: uncontrolled desire tyrannizes man's nature (a person's whole character can be warped by one overpowering feature)
take upon...yours: succeed to the throne
Convey: secretly arrange
spacious: lavish
seem cold...hoodwink: you can fool the world into thinking that you are pure
vulture: ravenous appetite
As will...inclined: who will offer themselves to a king when he so desires
ill-composed affection: unbalanced temperament
staunchless avarice: greed that cannot be satisfied

More suffer, and more sundry ways than ever,
By him that shall succeed.

MACDUFF   What should he be?

MALCOLM   It is myself I mean; in whom I know   50
All the particulars of vice so grafted,
That when they shall be opened, black Macbeth
Will seem as pure as snow, and the poor state
Esteem him as a lamb, being compared
With my confineless harms.

MACDUFF   Not in the legions
Of horrid hell can come a devil more damned
In evils, to top Macbeth.

MALCOLM   I grant him bloody,
Luxurious, avaricious, false, deceitful,
Sudden, malicious, smacking of every sin
That has a name. But there's no bottom, none,   60
in my voluptuousness. Your wives, your daughters,
Your matrons, and your maids, could not fill up
The cistern of my lust, and my desire
All continent impediments would o'erbear,
That did oppose my will. Better Macbeth
Than such a one to reign.

MACDUFF   Boundless intemperance
In nature is a tyranny; it hath been
Th' untimely emptying of the happy throne,
And fall of many kings. But fear not yet
To take upon you what is yours: you may   70
Convey your pleasures in a spacious plenty,
And yet seem cold, the time you may so hoodwink.
We have willing dames enough; there cannot be
That vulture in you, to devour so many
As will to greatness dedicate themselves,
Finding it so inclined.

MALCOLM   With this, there grows
In my most ill-composed affection, such
A staunchless avarice, that were I King,

Macduff is more concerned about Malcolm's self-confessed greed, but he says that, too, can be overcome. However, when Malcolm claims that he has no kingly qualities at all, Macduff is in utter despair.

---

cut off: kill
his: that man's
forge: make up
Sticks deeper: (see Act 3 scene 1 line 50)
grows with...root: develops from a more threatening basis (is fundamentally more threatening)
summer-seeming: summer-like (hot but short-lived)
sword...kings: reason for the death of Scottish kings who have been murdered
foisons: abundant supplies
mere own: own possessions
portable: bearable
With other...weighed: balanced against your other qualities
king-becoming graces: qualities which a king should have
As justice...fortitude: (James I studied the theory of kingship. This list, and the negative list in lines 57–59, would please him.)
verity: truth
temp'rance: moderation
Bounty: generosity
lowliness: humility
fortitude: reliability
relish: trace
division...crime: variations on every sort of evil
concord: harmony
confound: disrupt
Pour...earth: (see also Act 1 scene 5 lines 17, 47–50; Act 4 scene 1 lines 52–60)
untitled: usurping, not king by right
Since that...issue: because the truest heir (Malcolm)
interdiction: exclusion (i.e. his own words have excluded him from the throne
blaspheme his breed: dishonour his parentage
Died...lived: lived each day holily, as if it were to be her last

I should cut off the nobles for their lands,
Desire his jewels and this other's house,   80
And my more-having would be as a sauce
To make me hunger more, that I should forge
Quarrels unjust against the good and loyal,
Destroying them for wealth.

MACDUFF   This avarice
Sticks deeper, grows with more pernicious root
Than summer-seeing lust; and it hath been
The sword of our slain kings; yet do not fear;
Scotland hath foisons to fill up your will,
Of your mere own. All these are portable,
With other graces weighed.   90

MALCOLM   But I have none. The king-becoming graces,
As justice, verity, temp'rance, stableness,
Bounty, perseverance, mercy, lowliness,
Devotion, patience, courage, fortitude,
I have no relish of them, but abound
In the division of each several crime,
Acting it many ways. Nay, had I power, I should
Pour the sweet milk of concord into hell,
Uproar the universal peace, confound
All unity on earth.

ACDUFF   O Scotland, Scotland!   100

MALCOLM   If such a one be fit to govern, speak.
I am as I have spoken.

MACDUFF   Fit to govern?
No, not to live. O nation miserable,
With an untitled tyrant bloody-sceptered,
When shalt thou see thy wholesome days again,
Since that the truest issue of thy throne
By his own interdiction stands accursed,
And does blaspheme his breed? Thy royal father
Was a most sainted King; the Queen that bore thee,
Oftener upon her knees than on her feet,   110
Died every day she lived. Fare thee well,

Macduff's reaction convinces Malcolm of his sincerity. Malcolm confesses that what he has said about himself is completely untrue, and merely a test of Macduff's loyalty. An army has been raised to fight Macbeth. Macduff is confused by this turn of events.

These evils...Scotland: the evils which you recite against yourself are the very same evils which Macbeth has, and they have driven me from Scotland

Child of integrity: which comes from honesty

black scruples: dark suspicions

trains: plots

modest wisdom...haste: ordinary commonsense warns me about being too quick to believe everything I am told

to thy direction: in your hands

Unspeak...nature: withdraw what I said against myself and renounce the vices I confessed as foreign to my character

Unknown to: had no relations with

was forsworn: deceitful

coveted: desired

Whither: where (to Scotland)

here-approach: arrival

Old Siward: (Earl of Northumberland)

at a point: fully prepared

the chance...quarrel: may our chance of success be as sure as the justice of our cause

at once: at the same time

reconcile: accept, take in

King: Edward the Confessor

stay: await

his cure: (Edward was said to have healing powers, inherited by his successors – of whom James I was one!)

malady: illness

convinces: confounds

These evils thou repeat'st upon thyself
Hath banished me from Scotland. O my breast,
Thy hope ends here.

MALCOLM   Macduff, this noble passion,
Child of integrity, hath from my soul
Wiped the black scruples, reconciled my thoughts
To thy good truth and honour. Devilish Macbeth
By many of these trains hath sought to win me
Into his power; and modest wisdom plucks me
From over-credulous haste; but God above   120
Deal between thee and me. For even now
I put myself to thy direction, and
Unspeak mine own detraction; here abjure
The taints and blames I laid upon myself,
For strangers to my nature. I am yet
Unknown to woman, never was forsworn,
Scarcely have coveted what was mine own,
At no time broke my faith, would not betray
The devil to his fellow, and delight
No less in truth than life. My first false
        speaking   130
Was this upon myself. What I am truly,
Is thine, and my poor country's, to command;
Whither indeed, before thy here-approach,
Old Siward, with ten thousand warlike men
Already at a point, was setting forth.
Now we'll together, and the chance of goodness
Be like our warranted quarrel. Why are you silent?

MACDUFF   Such welcome and unwelcome things at once
'Tis hard to reconcile.

Enter a DOCTOR

MALCOLM   Well, more anon. Comes the King forth, I pray
        you?   140

DOCTOR   Ay sir, there are a crew of wretched souls
That stay his cure. Their malady convinces

**Malcolm explains the English king's powers of healing.
Ross arrives with news from Scotland.**

assay of art: efforts of medical science

presently amend: are cured instantly

the evil: scrofula, or the king's evil (a disease in which swollen
glands break through the skin)

here-remain: stay

solicits heaven: gets help from heaven

strangely-visited: extraordinarily afflicted

mere: complete

stamp: coin

'tis spoken: it is said

healing benediction: blessed gift of healing

virtue: power

heavenly...prophecy: (Edward's supernatural powers contrast
sharply with those of the witches)

sundry: various

grace: divine grace

I know him not: I do not recognize him/I do not know if he
is friend or foe

I know him now: (Macduff's welcome for Ross has reassured
Malcolm)

betimes: quickly

means: obstacles (Macbeth/Macbeth's habit of trying to trap
him)

Stands Scotland where it did?: Is the situation in Scotland
the same as it was before?

mother/grave: (contrast)

nothing But...smile: only the ignorant/idiots can smile

nothing: no-one

once: at any time

rent: rend, pierce

The great assay of art; but at his touch,
Such sanctity hath heaven given his hand,
They presently amend.

MALCOLM   I thank you doctor.

                                        [*Exit* DOCTOR

MACDUFF   What's the disease he means?

MALCOLM   'Tis called the evil:
A most miraculous work in this good King,
Which often since my here-remain in England
I have seen him do. How he solicits heaven,
Himself best knows; but strangely-visited
    people,   150
All swollen and ulcerous, pitiful to the eye,
The mere despair of surgery, he cures,
Hanging a golden stamp about their necks.
Put on with holy prayers; and 'tis spoken,
To the succeeding royalty he leaves
The healing benediction. With this strange virtue,
He hath a heavenly gift of prophecy,
And sundry blessings hang about his throne,
That speak him full of grace.

Enter ROSS

MACDUFF   See, who comes here?

MALCOLM   My countryman; but yet I know him not.   160

MACDUFF   My ever-gentle cousin, welcome hither.

MALCOLM   I know him now. Good God, betimes remove
The means that makes us strangers.

ROSS   Sir, amen.

MACDUFF   Stands Scotland where it did?

ROSS   Alas, poor country!
Almost afraid to know itself. It cannot
Be called our mother, but our grave; where nothing
But who knows nothing is once seen to smile;
Where sighs, and groans, and shrieks that rent the air,

Ross's news is of a Scotland suffering under Macbeth's evil control. Macduff asks Ross about Lady Macduff and his children, but Ross is evasive to begin with.

marked: remarked upon

modern ecstasy: everyday feeling, (ecstasy usually means a form of excitement or an extreme emotion, but, says Ross, such feelings are now commonplace)

The dead...who: people hardly bother asking for whom the funeral bell is ringing

Dying...sicken: killed before they have time to be ill

relation Too nice: the story is too detailed

newest: latest

That of... speaker: the person who tells of something which happened an hour previously is criticized (because the news is old)

teems: gives birth to

well/Well/well at peace: (play on words – Ross delays giving Macduff the news of his family and equivocates with the word '*well*'. Macbeth would understand Ross's '*well at peace*': see Act 3 scene 2 lines 22–23.)

niggard: miser

tidings...borne: (news of the deaths of Macduff's family)

out: had left home (to oppose Macbeth)

For that: because

power a-foot: army preparing

of help: for help

your eye: your presence seen

doff: throw off

England: King of England (also line 43)

gives out: tells of

Would I: I wish

That would: which ought to

latch: catch

	Are made, not marked; where violent sorrow seems	
	A modern ecstasy. The dead man's knell	170
	Is there scarce asked for who, and good men's lives	
	Expire before the flowers in their caps,	
	Dying or ere they sicken.	

MACDUFF   O relation
Too nice, and yet too true!

MALCOLM   What's the newest grief?

ROSS   That of an hour's age doth hiss the speaker.
Each minute teems a new one.

MACDUFF   How does my wife?

ROSS   Why, well.

MACDUFF   And all my children?

ROSS   Well too.

MACDUFF   The tyrant has not battered at their peace?

ROSS   No, they were well at peace, when I did leave 'em.

MACDUFF   Be not a niggard of your speech. How goes't?   180

ROSS   When I came hither to transport the tidings,
Which I have heavily borne, there ran a rumour
Of many worthy fellows that were out;
Which was to my belief witnessed the rather,
For that I saw the tyrant's power a-foot.
Now is the time of help; your eye in Scotland
Would create soldiers, make our women fight,
To doff their dire distresses.

MALCOLM   Be't their comfort
We are coming thither. Gracious England hath
Lent us good Siward, and ten thousand men;   190
An older and a better soldier none
That Christendom gives out.

ROSS   Would I could answer
This comfort with the like. But I have words
That would be howled out in the desert air,
When hearing should not latch them.

Ross gives Macduff the news of the murders. Macduff is stunned and seems unable to understand that it can have happened. Malcolm urges him to be angry and talk of revenge.

general cause: relating to everyone
fee-grief: sorrow concerning one particular person
Pertains to: concerns
possess: inform
To relate the manner: to tell you how it was done
quarry: heap of dead bodies (of deer)
deer: (play on words *deer/dear*)
Whispers...heart: whispers to the over-burdened heart
must be: had to be
Let us...grief: revenge will be like a medicine; doing the same to Macbeth will cure sorrow
He has no children:
    1 Macbeth has no children (and so revenge cannot be taken/he cannot understand what losing a family means) or
    2 Malcolm has no children (and is making a suggestion no father would make/he cannot understand how I feel)
hell-kite: bird of prey from hell
dam: mother
fell swoop: cruel attack (swoop of a bird of prey)

MACDUFF   What concern they?
        The general cause? Or is it a fee-grief
        Due to some single breast?

ROSS   No mind that's honest
        But in it shares some woe; though the main part
        Pertains to you alone.

MACDUFF   If it be mine,
        Keep it not from me, quickly let me have it.   200

ROSS   Let not your ears despise my tongue for ever,
        Which shall possess them with the heaviest sound
        That ever yet they heard.

MACDUFF   Hum! I guess at it.

ROSS   Your castle is surprised; your wife and babes
        Savagely slaughtered. To relate the manner,
        Were on the quarry of these murdered deer
        To add the death of you.

MALCOLM   Merciful heaven!
        What! man; ne'er pull your hat upon your brows,
        Give sorrow words; the grief that does not speak
        Whispers the o'er-fraught heart, and bids it
              break.   210

MACDUFF   My children too?

ROSS   Wife, children, servants, all
        That could be found.

MACDUFF   And I must be from thence!
        My wife killed too!

ROSS   I have said.

MALCOLM   Be comforted.
        Let's make us medicines of our great revenge,
        To cure this deadly grief.

MACDUFF   He has no children. All my pretty ones?
        Did you say all? O hell-kite! All?
        What, all my pretty chickens and their dam
        At one fell swoop?

Macduff blames himself for his family's deaths. He promises to settle his score with Macbeth when they meet on the battlefield. They leave to join up with the English forces and march to Scotland.

Dispute: fight against
take their part: act on their behalf
Sinful Macduff: (his family has been punished for his mistakes)
Naught: evil
demerits: faults
whetstone: means of sharpening
Convert: change
blunt not...enrage it: be angry, not depressed
braggart: boaster
intermission: delay
Front to front: face to face
Heaven...too: may God have mercy on his soul
tune: way of speaking
King: King Edward
power: army
Our lack...leave: all we need to do is to take our leave
ripe: ready (like a fruit tree)
powers above: angels, good spirits
Put on their instruments: arm themselves
cheer: comfort

ACTIVITIES

Keeping track

Scene 2

1 How does Lady Macduff react to the news that her husband has gone to England?

MALCOLM	Dispute it like a man.
MACDUFF	I shall do so; 220

But I must also feel it as a man:
I cannot but remember such things were
That were most precious to me. Did heaven look
       on,
And would not take their part? Sinful Macduff,
They were all struck for thee. Naught that I am,
Not for their own demerits, but for mine,
Fell slaughter on their souls. Heaven rest them now.

MALCOLM   Be this the whetstone of your sword, let grief
Convert to anger; blunt not the heart,
       enrage it.

MACDUFF   O I could play the woman with mine eyes,   230
And braggart with my tongue. But gentle heavens,
Cut short all intermission. Front to front
Bring thou this fiend of Scotland and myself;
Within my sword's length set him, if he 'scape,
Heaven forgive him too.

MALCOLM   This tune goes manly.
Come go we to the King; our power is ready,
Our lack is nothing but our leave. Macbeth
Is ripe for shaking, and the powers above
Put on their instruments. Receive what cheer you
       may,
The night is long that never finds the day.   240

                                        [*Exeunt*

2 What warning does the messenger bring?

Scene 3

3 Why is Malcolm suspicious of Macduff?

4 According to Malcolm, how will Scotland be worse off if he is king?

5 Why does Malcolm make his 'confessions' to Macduff?

6 How do Macduff's reactions to his family's murders first disappoint Malcolm and then satisfy him?

Discussion

1 • 'Act 4 Scene 2 is the only occasion in the play when the audience is given a glimpse of a loving family relationship'
  • 'The portrayal of the relationship between Lady Macduff and her son is nauseating. It is sickly sweet and utterly unconvincing. It is a relief when they are killed off.'
  Which of these two points of view do you support, and why?

2 Lady Macduff believes that Macduff has betrayed his family by leaving them and going to England. Do you think that she is justified in feeling this way? What would Macduff say in his own defence? Had he, for instance, any reason to anticipate what would happen to his family?

Drama

1 Divide the class into two groups, A and B.
  Group A
  Imagine you work for Macbeth's press office, and need to explain the murders of Macduff's family:
  • write the press release
  • produce the photographs (using still image convention, see FREEZE! page 227)
  • prepare the television announcement (with pictures).
  Will you want Macbeth or Lady Macbeth to say anything or appear on television?
  Group B
  Imagine you are working for Malcolm's press office. Do the same as Group A. You will be unable to have the

cooperation of Macbeth or Lady Macbeth, but you might be able to edit some of Group A's material – if you can get hold of it! Will you want some quotations or an appearance from Malcolm and Donalbain? What about the '*pious English King, Edward*'?

2 Malcolm commissions a painting to be called 'The Massacre of the Innocents', which will show the murder of the Macduff family. Imagine you have been asked to do this painting. Create the image. Present it to Malcolm. As artists, how do you feel about such a commission? How do you think Macduff would feel if he were invited by Malcolm to see the painting?

3 Scene 3 is a long and potentially tedious scene, which is mainly a dialogue between two men. Work in groups of five or six. Imagine that you are involved in making a film of this scene. Decide what sort of location you need, and then create the storyboard for the cameraman.

Use a variety of cinematic effects, such as long shots, close-ups, cuts, panning, zooming, bird's eye and from the floor. You will need to decide on the moves and be able to justify them from the text.

Character

1 In scene 3 we learn much more about the rightful King of Scotland, Malcolm.
   a What characteristics are evident in lines 8–31 and 37–44?
   b Look again quickly at lines 50–102, and in more detail at lines 114–137. What does this show us about Malcolm's character? Has he handled Macduff's visit wisely?
   c In the last part of the scene, from Ross's entrance to the end, how does Malcolm show both maturity and immaturity?

2 After hearing what Lady Macduff and Ross think about him in scene 2 we learn much more about Macduff in scene 3. What can we say about him from the way in which he reacts to
   • Malcolm's suspicions
   • Malcolm's 'confessions'
   • the news of his family's slaughter?

3 Bring your CHARACTER LOGS up to date.

Close study

1 The English doctor appears at line 139 of scene 3 and goes out at line 145, having spoken four and a half lines. What is Shakespeare's purpose in introducing this character? Could it be for dramatic reasons (see DISCUSSION 1, page 79)? Perhaps he is included so that Edward the Confessor can be mentioned. (Why might Shakespeare want to do that?)

2 Some productions of the play do not include scene 3 because it is argued that this scene slows down the action without adding much to the audience's awareness.

    a What purpose do you think scene 3 serves? At the end of the scene:

      • how do the audience feel about Malcolm?

      • how do the audience feel about Macduff?

      • how has the plot of the play moved on?

    b Imagine that you are directing a production of *Macbeth* and that you wish to make scene 3 shorter. Look through the text and suggest which lines you would take out.

Writing

1 In many ways Shakespeare is concerned with what makes a good king. Look again at scene 2 and, especially, scene 3, to see what he has to say, directly and indirectly, about kingly qualities.

    Make two lists: one list of the qualities a king should have, and the other of the qualities a king should *not* have. Alongside each quality write the letter 'D' if Shakespeare says this directly, or 'I' if it is indirectly suggested (i.e. you have worked it out for yourself from the action or the dialogue of the play). Compare your lists with others in the group.

2 Let us assume that the murderers of Lady Macduff are the same people responsible for Banquo's murder. It is quite

likely that in the meantime they have performed other similar deeds for Macbeth. In order to commission them to carry out this latest murder, Macbeth had to send them a message. We heard what Macbeth had to say to these men in Act 3 scene 1, and we know how he received news of Banquo's death in Act 3 scene 4. What would a written message to them contain on this occasion? Write Macbeth's message.

Quiz

Who said the following, and to whom?
1 '*For even now*
   I put myself to thy direction'
2 '*Your castle is surprised; your wife and babes*
   Savagely slaughtered'
3 '*Dispute it like a man*'

Who said the following, and about whom?
4 '*He loves us not;*
   He wants the natural touch'
5 '*He is noble, wise, judicious, and best knows*
   The fits o' th' season'
6 '*This tyrant, whose sole name blisters out tongues,*
   Was once thought honest'

Who said the following, when, and about what?
7 '*Whither should I fly?*
   I have done no harm'
8 '*If such a one be fit to govern, speak.*
   I am as I have spoken'
9 '*What I am truly,*
   Is thine, and my poor country's, to command'

Who said the following, when, and about what? Comment on the imagery.
10 '*For the poor wren,*
    The most diminutive of birds, will fight,
    Her young ones in her nest, against the owl'

Lady Macbeth's lady-in-waiting has called a doctor to watch her mistress's sleepwalking. For two nights Lady Macbeth has not stirred, but now she enters, carrying a candle.

The notes on this scene contain numerous references to earlier parts of the play. It is not necessary to look up each reference at your first reading, but you might find them useful for written work later on.

field: battlefield (against the rebels, Act 4 scene 3 line 183)
nightgown: dressing-gown (as Act 2 scene 2 line 67)
closet: a cabinet or chest for papers
perturbation in nature: disturbance in her well-being (the doctor speaks in a pompous manner; perhaps he feels it is fitting to his position)
effects of watching: things she would do when awake
slumbery agitation: activity whilst asleep
actual performances: acts
I will not: I absolutely refuse to (she is wisely cautious)
meet: proper
guise: way she appears
close: hidden
'tis her command: (and yet Lady Macbeth called for darkness, Act 1 scene 5 lines 50–55)

Act five

Scene

Macbeth's castle

Enter a DOCTOR OF PHYSIC *and a* WAITING
GENTLEWOMAN

DOCTOR	I have two nights watched with you, but can perceive no truth in your report. When was it she last walked?
GENTLE.	Since his Majesty went into the field, I have seen her rise from her bed, throw her nightgown upon her, unlock her closet, take forth paper, fold it, write upon't, read it, afterwards seal it, and again return to bed; yet all this while in a most fast sleep.
DOCTOR	A great perturbation in nature, to receive at once the benefit of sleep, and do the effects of watching. In this slumbery agitation, besides her walking, and other actual performances, what at any time have you heard her say?
GENTLE.	That sir, which I will not report after her.
DOCTOR	You may to me, and 'tis most meet you should.
GENTLE.	Neither to you nor any one, having no witness to confirm my speech.

10

Enter LADY MACBETH *with a taper*

Lo you, here she comes. This is her very guise, and
upon my life, fast asleep.
Observe her, stand close.   20

DOCTOR	How came she by that light?
GENTLE.	Why it stood by her. She has light by her continually, 'tis her command.

Lady Macbeth seems to be washing her hands, and then she begins speaking. The doctor is alarmed by what he hears: references to the deaths of Duncan and Lady Macduff, and, unknown to him, the death of Banquo.

---

sense: (plural) powers of sight
Yet: even now, after all this washing
spot: stain
Yet...spot: (see Act 2 scene 2 lines 43–44, 57–58 and especially 64)
set down: write down
satisfy: support
One, two: (the signal for Duncan's murder, Act 2 scene 1 lines 31–32, 62)
A soldier, and afeard?: (see Act 1 scene 7 lines 39–41, 49)
none can...account: (see Act 1 scene 7 lines 77–79)
Yet who...him?: (see Act 2 scene 2 lines 52–53, 61)
The Thane...now?: (Lady Macbeth is well aware of her husband's responsibility for the deaths of Macduff's family)
No more...starting: (see Act 3 scene 4 line 63)
Go to: indeed
You/you: (Lady Macbeth)
all the perfumes of Arabia: (compare Act 2 scene 2 lines 57–58)
Oh! oh! oh!: (this probably represents one long sigh)
sorely charged: painfully burdened
dignity: worth

DOCTOR	You see her eyes are open.
GENTLE.	Ay but their sense is shut.
DOCTOR	What is it she does now? Look how she rubs her hands.
GENTLE.	It is an accustomed action with her, to seem thus washing her hands. I have known her continue in this a quarter of an hour. 30
L. MACBETH	Yet here's a spot.
DOCTOR	Hark! she speaks. I will set down what comes from her, to satisfy my remembrance the more strongly.
L. MACBETH	Out damned spot, out I say! One, two; why then 'tis time to do't. Hell is murky. Fie my lord, fie! A soldier, and afeard? What need we fear who knows it, when none can call our power to account? Yet who would have thought the old man to have had so much blood in him? 40
DOCTOR	Do you mark that?
L. MACBETH	The Thane of Fife had a wife; where is she now? What, will these hands ne'er be clean? No more o' that my lord, no more o' that: you mar all with this starting.
DOCTOR	Go to, go to! You have known what you should not.
GENTLE.	She has spoke what she should not, I am sure of that. Heaven knows what she has known.
L. MACBETH	Here's the smell of the blood still; all the 50 perfumes of Arabia will not sweeten this little hand. Oh, oh, oh!
DOCTOR	What a sigh is there! The heart is sorely charged.
GENTLE.	I would not have such a heart in my bosom for the dignity of the whole body.
DOCTOR	Well, well, well.
GENTLE.	Pray God it be sir.

The doctor says that Lady Macbeth needs a priest rather than a doctor and he warns the gentlewoman to keep an eye on her mistress, making sure that she has no means of harming herself.

practice: medical skill
I have...beds: (in Shakespeare's time sleepwalking was thought to mean that the person was possessed by demons)
Wash...nightgown: (see Act 2 scene 2 lines 64, 67)
look...pale: (see Act 3 scene 4 lines 115–116)
I tell...grave: (see Act 3 scene 4 lines 80–82)
on's: of his
Even so?: What? There's more?
To bed...gate: (see Act 2 scene 2 lines 62–63)
Come...hand: (The probable ending of Act 2 scene 2; see page 58.)
What's done...undone: (see Act 3 scene 2 line 12)
Foul...abroad: rumours of evil are widespread
infected: corrupted
divine: priest (for her soul)
means of all annoyance: means of injuring herself
still: always
mated: bewildered

Scottish forces are gathering to join up with the English army, led by Macduff, Malcolm and Siward.

power: army
uncle: (Historically, Siward was Duncan's father-in-law, and therefore Malcolm's grandfather. Shakespeare has made Duncan older for dramatic purposes, and so, for consistency, Siward becomes Malcolm's uncle.)

DOCTOR	This disease is beyond my practice. Yet I have known those which have walked in their sleep who have died holily in their beds. 60
L. MACBETH	Wash your hands, put on your nightgown, look not so pale. I tell you yet again Banquo's buried; he cannot come out on's grave.
DOCTOR	Even so?
L. MACBETH	To bed, to bed; there's knocking at the gate. Come, come, come, come, give me your hand. What's done cannot be undone. To bed, to bed, to bed.
	[*Exit*
DOCTOR	Will she go now to bed?
GENTLE.	Directly. 70
DOCTOR	Foul whisperings are abroad. Unnatural deeds Do breed unnatural troubles; infected minds To their deaf pillows will discharge their secrets. More needs she the divine than the physician. God, God forgive us all. Look after her, Remove from her the means of all annoyance, And still keep eyes upon her. So, good night: My mind she has mated, and amazed my sight. I think, but dare not speak.
GENTLE.	Good night, good doctor.
	[*Exeunt*

Scene

Near Dunsinane

Enter, with drum and colours, MENTEITH,
CAITHNESS, ANGUS, LENNOX, *and* SOLDIERS

MENTEITH	The English power is near, led on by Malcolm, His uncle Siward, and the good Macduff.

By this time Macbeth is almost without support: only mercenaries stand with him. The Scots move on to Birnam to meet Malcolm's forces.

Revenges: desire for revenge

dear causes: deeply-felt reasons (for revenge)

to the...man: rouse the dead to respond to the call to arms

well: probably

LENNOX: (He distrusted Macbeth in Act 3 scene 6, but was with him at the cavern, Act 4 scene 1. He is now certainly a '*rebel*'.)

file: list

unrough: unshaved (not old enough to shave)

Protest...manhood: show for the first time that they are grown men (taking part in their first battle). They were regarded as men when they were strong enough to carry armour and wield a sword. Twenty-one was considered to be the right age.

buckle...rule: he cannot control his frenzied behaviour/he cannot prevent his subjects from rebelling against this corruption

buckle/belt: (clothing imagery)

sticking: (like blood)

Now does...hands: (see Act 2 scene 2 line 56)

Now minutely...faith-breach: now every minute desertions denounce his treason

only in command: only because they are ordered to

thief: (he stole the king's title)

Now does...thief: (clothing imagery; see Act 1 scene 3 lines 108–109, 145)

pestered: troubled

recoil and start: (see Act 3 scene 4 line 63; Act 5 scene 1 lines 44–45)

all that...there: all aspects of his own nature revolt against him

where 'tis truly owed: (to Malcolm)

medicine: cure

sickly weal: sick land (commonwealth)

pour we...us: we will shed every drop of blood to purify our country ('bleeding' was a cure for many illnesses)

dew: water

sovereign flower: royal flower (Malcolm)/a medicinal herb

Revenges burn in them; for their dear causes
Would to the bleeding and the grim alarm
Excite the mortified man.

ANGUS   Near Birnam wood
Shall we well meet them; that way are they coming.

CAITHNESS   Who knows if Donalbain be with his brother?

LENNOX   For certain sir, he is not. I have a file
Of all the gentry; there is Siward's son,
And many unrough youths, that even now   10
Protest their first of manhood.

MENTEITH   What does the tyrant?

CAITHNESS   Great Dunsinane he strongly fortifies.
Some say he's mad; others, that lesser hate him,
Do call it valiant fury; but for certain,
He cannot buckle his distempered cause
Within the belt of rule.

ANGUS   Now does he feel
His secret murders sticking on his hands.
Now minutely revolts upbraid his faith-breach;
Those he commands move only in command,
Nothing in love. Now does he feel his title   20
Hang loose about him, like a giant's robe
Upon a dwarfish thief.

MENTEITH   Who then shall blame
His pestered senses to recoil and start,
When all that is within him does condemn
Itself for being there?

CAITHNESS   Well, march we on,
To give obedience where 'tis truly owed.
Meet we the medicine of the sickly weal,
And with him pour we, in our country's purge,
Each drop of us.

LENNOX   Or so much as it needs,
To dew the sovereign flower, and drown the weeds. 30
Make we our march towards Birnam.

                                   [*Exeunt, marching*

Macbeth is extremely agitated. He is loudly confident of success because of what the apparitions have said, but his violent scorn towards the servant shows that he is ill-at-ease.

---

let them fly all: let all my thanes desert me

taint: be weakened

The spirits...consequences: the apparitions which know how earthly things will turn out

epicures: self-indulgent weaklings (*epicure* – person who delights in feasting)

sway: control myself

sag: droop

The mind...fear: (rhyming couplet to end this train of thought)

The devil...black: Go to the devil! (Devils were supposed to be black.)

cream-faced loon: pasty-faced rogue

goose: bird/fool/woman of loose morals/prostitute

goose look: appearance of goose-flesh/heavily powdered appearance

over-red: paint over with blood

lily-livered: cowardly (the liver was thought to be the seat of courage; a bloodless/pale liver was the sign of a coward)

patch: clown (with white face)

Death...soul: your spirit has gone

linen: (white, again)

counsellors to fear: put fear in the minds of others

whey: liquid left after the milk has curdled (It is white!)

Seyton!...I say!: (Macbeth calls for his personal servant, and then lapses into depression)

push: crisis

Scene 3

Macbeth's castle

Enter MACBETH, DOCTOR, *and* ATTENDANTS

MACBETH   Bring me no more reports, let them fly all.
Till Birnam wood remove to Dunsinane,
I cannot taint with fear. What's the boy Malcolm?
Was he not born of woman? The spirits that know
All mortal consequences have pronounced me thus:
'Fear not Macbeth, no man that's born of woman
Shall e'er have power upon thee.' Then fly false thanes,
And mingle with the English epicures.
The mind I sway by, and the heart I bear,
Shall never sag with doubt, nor shake with fear.   10

Enter a SERVANT

The devil damn thee black, thou cream-faced loon.
Where gott'st thou that goose look?

SERVANT   There is ten thousand –

MACBETH   Geese, villain?

SERVANT   Soldiers sir.

MACBETH   Go prick thy face, and over-red thy fear,
Thou lily-livered boy. What soldiers, patch?
Death of thy soul, those linen cheeks of thine
Are counsellors to fear. What soldiers, whey-face?

SERVANT   The English force, so please you.

MACBETH   Take thy face hence.   [*Exit* SERVANT
                Seyton! – I am sick at heart,
When I behold – Seyton, I say! – This push   20

Macbeth regrets a lack of true friends, but he is soon talking defiantly about fighting to the death. The doctor tells him that Lady Macbeth's sickness is not a medical condition.

cheer: hearten (play on words – *cheer/chair*, throne)
disseat: dethrone
sear: dry, withered state
As: such as
stead: place
mouth-honour: lip service (apparent friendship)
breath: mere air
fain deny: gladly withhold
I'll put it on: (Macbeth's indecisiveness with his armour indicates his troubled mind)
moe horses: more horsemen
skirr: scour
Hang those...fear: (he does not accept that he has no influence now)
your patient: Lady Macbeth
thick-coming fancies: teeming delusions
minister to: treat (also, help spiritually)
rooted: firmly established
Raze out...brain: rub out the troubles imprinted on the mind
oblivious: bringing forgetfulness
stuffed bosom: overburdened heart
perilous stuff: sorrow
Therein...himself: the cure is in the patient's hands (i.e. you are talking about conscience)
himself: (the doctor suspects that Macbeth has been asking about his own needs as well as those of his wife)
physic: medicine
I'll none of it: I'll have nothing to do with it (James I would like this because they were his sentiments.)

Will cheer me ever, or disseat me now.
I have lived long enough. My way of life
Is fallen into the sear, the yellow leaf;
And that which should accompany old age,
As honour, love, obedience, troops of friends,
I must not look to have; but in their stead
Curses, not loud but deep, mouth-honour, breath
Which the poor heart would fain deny, and dare
   not.
Seyton!

Enter SEYTON

SEYTON   What's your gracious pleasure?

MACBETH   What news more?   30

SEYTON   All is confirmed my lord, which was reported.

MACBETH   I'll fight, till from my bones my flesh be hacked.
Give me my armour.

SEYTON   'Tis not needed yet.

MACBETH   I'll put it on.
Send out more horses, skirr the country round,
Hang those that talk of fear. Give me mine armour.
How does your patient, doctor?

DOCTOR   Not so sick my lord,
As she is troubled with thick-coming fancies
That keep her from her rest.

MACBETH   Cure her of that.
Canst thou not minister to a mind diseased,   40
Pluck from the memory a rooted sorrow,
Raze out the written troubles of the brain,
And with some sweet oblivious antidote
Cleanse the stuffed bosom of that perilous stuff
Which weighs upon the heart?

DOCTOR   Therein the patient
Must minister to himself.

MACBETH   Throw physic to the dogs, I'll none of it.

Macbeth asks the doctor to find a cure for Scotland:
something to get rid of the English army. He is still
undecided about whether to wear his armour.

---

staff: commander's baton
sir: (Macbeth addresses Seyton, who is helping him into his
    armour)
dispatch: hurry
cast The water: diagnose the disease by testing urine
purge: cleanse, clear it out
pristine: former
Pull't off: (a change of mind about the armour)
rhubarb, senna: plants known for their laxative properties
purge it...English hence: (see Act 5 scene 2 lines 27–29)
Hear'st thou of them?: Have you heard about the English?
it: the armour
bane: destruction
Profit...here: I would not come back here if you paid me!

ACTIVITIES

Keeping track

Scene 1

1 What has the gentlewoman reported to the doctor?
2 What action is Lady Macbeth performing with her hands?
3 Whose murders does Lady Macbeth speak about?

Scene 2

4 Where will the Scots meet up with the English army?

Scene 3

5 Which messages from the apparitions give Macbeth hope,
   even in the situation in which he finds himself?
6 Why is the doctor unable to help Lady Macbeth?

          Come, put mine armour on; give me my staff.
          Seyton, send out. Doctor, the thanes fly from me.
          Come sir, dispatch. If thou couldst, doctor, cast   50
          The water of my land, find her disease,
          And purge it to a sound and pristine health,
          I would applaud thee to the very echo,
          That should applaud again. Pull't off I say.
          What rhubarb, senna, or what purgative drug,
          Would scour these English hence? Hear'st thou of
            them?

DOCTOR   Ay my good lord; your royal preparation
          Makes us hear something.

MACBETH   Bring it after me.
          I will not be afraid of death and bane,
          Till Birnam forest come to Dunsinane.   60
                     [*Exeunt all but* DOCTOR

DOCTOR   Were I from Dunsinane away, and clear,
          Profit again should hardly draw me here.

Discussion

1 We are told by the gentlewoman that Lady Macbeth writes
  during her sleepwalking. What do you think she can be
  writing about?

2 When you think back, have there been warning signs that
  Lady Macbeth has been heading for a breakdown? Do you
  think that there is anything in particular which has brought it
  on? Do you have any thoughts about what might happen to
  Lady Macbeth in the future?

3 In scene 2 Lennox is seen with the Scottish army opposed to
  Macbeth. What reasons might he give for staying with
  Macbeth for so long when others had defected much earlier?

4 When asked whether Donalbain is with Malcolm's forces, Lennox replies, '*For certain sir, he is not. I have a file Of all the gentry*' (scene 2 lines 8–9)

From this, what can we assume about the way in which Malcolm's army is run? How does this compare with what we learn of Macbeth's preparations for battle in the following scene?

5 The doctor enters with Macbeth at the beginning of scene 3, but is not spoken to until line 37.

   a Why is this? Does Macbeth not care about Lady Macbeth's health? Is he too busy with other things?

   b During the course of those early lines, what will the doctor be doing? Will he be hovering close to Macbeth, waiting to be spoken to? Will he be keeping out of the way, hoping that Macbeth has forgotten him?

Drama

'Brought in for questioning'

Imagine that the battle is over and Lady Macbeth has been captured and imprisoned. Malcolm has sent Ross to collect evidence of witchcraft and treachery. Ross has collected two written statements:

- the speech made by Lady Macbeth (Act 5 scene 1 lines 35–40) which was overheard by an attendant
- the doctor's record of the events of Act 5 scene 1.

1 Work in small groups

You are the prosecuting officers who are to be given this evidence. The attendant, the doctor and the gentlewoman will be available for questioning. You could also visit Lady Macbeth and interview her.

Decide what questions you would like to ask her.

2 Work in a larger group

Roles: Ross, the doctor, the gentlewoman, possibly Lady Macbeth, the prosecuting officers (as above)

The prosecuting officers (with Ross in charge, but in the

background) now question their witnesses. They may even
want to interview certain of them more than once.

Follow up

Having gathered the evidence you could then conduct the trial.
Remember that Malcolm sees this as a show trial, so that if you
decide that she is not guilty then you will have some explaining to
do. What defence could she have? Would she conduct her own
defence?

Character

1 **a** Would it be fair to say that Lady Macbeth wins some
sympathy from the audience in the sleep-walking scene
(scene 1)? Why? In general terms, what does the scene
reveal about her?

b More particularly, Lady Macbeth says at line 42 '*The Thane
of Fife had a wife; where is she now?*' What does the rhythm of
this line suggest to you? What impression do you get of her
state of mind from this line? Find other quotations which
give a clue to different aspects of her mental health. The
clue might be in what she says, or in the language she uses
to say it – or both. What do these quotations tell us about
her?

2 **a** In scene 3 what mood is Macbeth in, in each of these
sections? lines 1–10; lines 11–19; lines 19–28; lines 30–36;
lines 40–45

b How many times does Macbeth change the topic of
conversation in lines 47–56? What does this tell us about his
general state of mind?

c Is it possible that even Macbeth might arouse some
sympathy in the audience during this scene? Can you
say why?

3 Bring your CHARACTER LOGS up to date.

Close study

1 Look at how scene 1 is written. Apart from the doctor's final
speech, it is in prose. After the emotional verse at the end of

Act 4 scene 3, the audience would certainly be aware of a change of pace here.

What feelings in the audience would the use of prose create: amusement, fear, expectation, boredom, excitement, sympathy?

2 What incidents in her life does Lady Macbeth mention in the sleep-walking scene?

Make a list of the events in the order in which Lady Macbeth speaks about them, and next to them number the events in chronological order (the order in which they happened). Why are they not mentioned in the order in which they happened?

3 What is the purpose of the very short scene 2? Does it take the plot forward? Does it reveal new aspects of any character? What does it do?

4 In scene 3 lines 19–28, Macbeth regrets his way of life, but shows no remorse for what he has done. What particularly does he regret?

Act 5 scenes 1 and 3 are said to emphasize the disorder for which the Macbeths are responsible. We have previously seen disorder in the natural world. (Can you remember when?) What sort of disorder is evident in these scenes? How does Shakespeare achieve this effect? Is it through actions or language – or both? Find examples from both scenes which best illustrate disorder.

Writing

1 In Scene 1 we see the doctor making notes on what Lady Macbeth does and says, and on what the gentlewoman has told him about her. We know from how he responds to what he has witnessed, and from his final speech, what his thoughts are. As the doctor, write your notes and finally add your own comments on the night's events. These comments are not intended to be seen by anyone else so you can be quite honest in what you write. (The comments can also be in note form, if you wish.)

2 'O, never Shall sun that morrow see' (Act 1 scene 5 lines 60–61)

'*keep eyes upon her*' (Act 5 scene 1 line 77).

Using your CHARACTER LOG, write about the ways in which Lady Macbeth changes during the course of the play.

- The 'body', or main part, of your essay will show how the determined woman of Act 1 scene 5 becomes the creature whom the doctor pities in Act 5 scene 1. Give reasons for the changes which take place.
- You will need to use quotations to illustrate the main points which you make.
- Begin the essay with a paragraph in which you comment on the first impression which Lady Macbeth makes
- End with a paragraph giving your opinion of her and the situation she is now in.

Quiz

Who said the following, and to whom?

1 '*You have known what you should not*'
2 '*The devil damn thee black, thou cream-faced loon*'
3 '*Come, put mine armour on; give me my staff*'

Who said the following, and about whom?

4 '*It is an accustomed action with her, to seem thus washing her hands*'
5 '*Great Dunsinane he strongly fortifies.
   Some say he's mad*'
6 '*she is troubled with thick-coming fancies
   That keep her from her rest*'

Who said the following, when, and about what?

7 '*Yet who would have thought the old man to have so much blood in him?*'
8 '*all the perfumes of Arabia will not sweeten this little hand*'
9 '*Look after her,
   Remove from her the means of all annoyance*'

Who said the following, when and about what? Comment on the imagery.

10 '*What rhubarb, senna, or what purgative drug,
   Would scour these English hence?*'

The English forces have met the Scots at Birnam Wood.
Malcolm orders them all to carry a branch from the trees
so that the enemy will not be able to see how many of
them there are. They know that more of Macbeth's men
have left him.

chambers will be safe: men will be safe in their beds (he is
    thinking of Duncan)
nothing: not at all
shadow: hide
host: army
discovery: Macbeth's scouts
no other but: no other news than
endure: hold out against
Our setting...before't: a siege by us
advantage: opportunity
more and...revolt: nobles and commoners have deserted him
constrained things: conscripted wretches
Let our...event: let us see if our opinions are accurate when
    the battle takes place
put we...soldiership: let us take full military precautions
due decision: the eventual outcome
What we...owe: what is our strength, and what we are lacking
Thoughts...relate: guesses may express false hopes

Scene  4

Birnam wood

Enter, with drum and colours, MALCOLM, SIWARD
and YOUNG SIWARD, MACDUFF, MENTEITH,
CAITHNESS, ANGUS, LENNOX, ROSS, *and* SOLDIERS,
marching

MALCOLM   Cousins, I hope the days are near at hand
That chambers will be safe.

MENTEITH   We doubt it nothing.

SIWARD   What wood is this before us?

MENTEITH   The wood of Birnam.

MALCOLM   Let every soldier hew him down a bough,
And bear't before him, thereby shall we shadow
The numbers of our host, and make discovery
Err in report of us.

SOLDIERS   It shall be done.

SIWARD   We learn no other but the confident tyrant
Keeps still in Dunsinane, and will endure
Our setting down before't.

MALCOLM   'Tis his main hope.   10
For where there is advantage to be gone,
Both more and less have given him the revolt,
And none serve with him but constrained things,
Whose hearts are absent too.

MACDUFF   Let our just censures
Attend the true event, and put we on
Industrious soldiership.

SIWARD   The time approaches
That will with due decision make us know
What we shall say we have, and what we owe.
Thoughts speculative their unsure hopes relate,

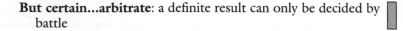

But certain...arbitrate: a definite result can only be decided by battle

Macbeth is confident that he can withstand a siege. Seyton brings him the news that Lady Macbeth is dead.

Hang out...walls: (to let them know we are here)
ague: fever
forced: reinforced
dareful...beard: boldly, face-to-face
The time has been: there was a time when
my senses...cooled: I would have gone cold
night-shriek: cry in the night
fell of hair: scalp
dismal treatise: horrifying story
As life were in't: as if it were alive
supped: (this suggests that he has been responsible for the horrors – they have not been thrust upon him; '*supped*' also brings to mind the supper or banquet, and Banquo's ghost)
Direness: horror
Cannot...me: can never frighten me now
hereafter: later, at a more fitting time
a time...word: a proper time to die
She should...word: (Macbeth's response gives rise to much discussion about his state of mind and his relationship with his wife)

But certain issue strokes must arbitrate;   20
Towards which advance the war.

[Exeunt, marching

Scene 5

Dunsinane

Enter, with drum and colours, MACBETH, SEYTON
and SOLDIERS

MACBETH   Hang out our banners on the outward walls.
The cry is still 'They come'. Our castle's strength
Will laugh a siege to scorn. Here let them lie
Till famine and the ague eat them up.
Were they not forced with those that should be
          ours,
We might have met them dareful, beard to beard,
And beat them backward home.

[A cry of women within
What is that noise?

SEYTON   It is the cry of women, my good lord.   *[Exit*

MACBETH   I have almost forgot the taste of fears.
The time has been, my senses would have
          cooled   10
To hear a night-shriek, and my fell of hair
Would at a dismal treatise rouse and stir
As life were in't. I have supped full with horrors;
Direness, familiar to my slaughterous thoughts,
Cannot once start me.

Enter SEYTON

Wherefore was that cry?

SEYTON   The Queen, my lord, is dead.

MACBETH   She should have died hereafter;
There would have been a time for such a word.

Macbeth reflects on the insignificance of life. A messenger reports that Birnam Wood is moving towards Dunsinane. Macbeth decides that there is no point in waiting or in running away, and he goes to meet the enemy.

Tomorrow...tomorrow: (a meaningless succession of days)
Creeps in...day: time is measured in this insignificant way
To the...time: until the book of life ends (Judgement Day)
all our yesterdays: every day in the past
all our...death: every day has shown (as with a light, candle) fools the way to the grave
brief candle: short-lived light (life)
Life's but...more: life is like a moving shadow, making no impression; or a bad actor who walks on stage and makes a great show of performing for a short time but is never heard of again
tale Told: completed story
sound and fury: words and emotion
Signifying nothing: it is meaningless
Tomorrow...nothing:
  1 biblical references – 'For we are but of yesterday, and are ignorant: for our days upon earth are but a shadow' *Job 8, 9* 'The light shall be dark in his dwelling, and his candle shall be put out with him' *Job 18, 6* 'We bring our years to an end as it were a tale that is told' *Psalms 90, 9*
  2 note images of: sound, movement, time, light, theatre
endure your wrath: put up with your anger
famine cling thee: you shrivel from starvation
sooth: truth
I pull in resolution: I draw back (weaken) in courage
fiend: devil
begin To doubt...truth: (see Act 2 scene 3 lines 8–11)
Arm...out!: (he decides to attack)
avouches: asserts, says
There is nor: there is no point in
tarrying: waiting, hanging about

Tomorrow, and tomorrow, and tomorrow,
Creeps in this petty pace from day to day,   20
To the last syllable of recorded time;
And all our yesterdays have lighted fools
The way to dusty death. Out, out, brief candle!
Life's but a walking shadow, a poor player,
That struts and frets his hour upon the stage,
And then is heard no more. It is a tale
Told by an idiot, full of sound and fury,
Signifying nothing.

Enter a MESSENGER

Thou comest to use thy tongue. Thy story quickly.

MESSENGER   Gracious my lord,   30
I should report that which I say I saw,
But know not how to do't.

MACBETH   Well, say, sir.

MESSENGER   As I did stand my watch upon the hill,
I looked toward Birnam, and anon methought
The wood began to move.

MACBETH   Liar and slave!

MESSENGER   Let me endure your wrath, if 't be not so.
Within this three mile may you see it coming.
I say, a moving grove.

MACBETH   If thou speak'st false,
Upon the next tree shalt thou hang alive
Till famine cling thee. If thy speech be sooth,   40
I care not if thou dost for me as much.
I pull in resolution, and begin
To doubt th' equivocation of the fiend,
That lies like truth: 'Fear not, till Birnam wood
Do come to Dunsinane'; and now a wood
Comes toward Dunsinane. Arm, arm, and out!
If this which he avouches does appear,
There is nor flying hence, nor tarrying here.

sun: day (the daily round)

and wish...undone: (if he is going to die he wants the whole world to be destroyed with him – see Act 3 scene 2 line 16; Act 4 scene 1 lines 58–60)

wrack: wreck

harness: armour

The attacking army throw down their branches, and Malcolm gives the order to begin fighting.

---

uncle: Old Siward

first battle: main army

we: (royal plural)

upon's: upon us

order: plan

Do we but: if we

power: troops

harbingers: heralds, messengers who go in front

Macbeth has no choice: he must fight.

---

tied...stake: (like a bear to be baited by dogs)

course: bout

What's he: What sort of man is he?

I 'gin to be aweary of the sun,
And wish th' estate o' th' world were now
    undone.   50
Ring the alarum bell! Blow wind, come wrack,
At least we'll die with harness on our back.

                                       [*Exeunt*

Scene 6

Before the castle

Enter, with drum and colours, MALCOLM, SIWARD,
MACDUFF, *etc., and their Army, with boughs*

MALCOLM   Now near enough; your leafy screens throw down,
And show like those you are. You, worthy uncle,
Shall with my cousin your right noble son,
Lead our first battle. Worthy Macduff and we
Shall take upon's what else remains to do.
According to our order.

SIWARD   Fare you well.
Do we but find the tyrant's power tonight,
Let us be beaten, if we cannot fight.

MACDUFF   Make all our trumpets speak, give them all breath,
Those clamorous harbingers of blood and death. 10

                              [*Exeunt. Alarums*

Scene 7

Before the castle

Alarums. Enter MACBETH

MACBETH   They have tied me to a stake; I cannot fly,
But bear-like I must fight the course. What's he
That was not born of woman? Such a one
Am I to fear, or none.

Macbeth kills Young Siward, but Macduff is getting close to him. Old Siward tells Malcolm that the castle has been taken.

---

abhorred: hateful, offensive
with my...speak'st: (as if it were trial by combat)
Brandished: wielded
swords I...born: (Macbeth's confidence is growing)
Thou be'st: you are
still: for ever
kerns: Irish mercenaries (such as Macdonwald employed, Act 1 scene 2)
staves: spears
undeeded: unused
By this great clatter: judging by this great noise
greatest note: most importance/notoriety (see page 96)
bruited: announced
gently rendered: readily surrendered
The day...yours: you have almost won the battle

Enter YOUNG SIWARD

Y. SIWARD	What is thy name?
MACBETH	Thou'lt be afraid to hear it.
Y. SIWARD	No; though thou call'st thyself a hotter name Than any is in hell.
MACBETH	My name's Macbeth.
Y. SIWARD	The devil himself could not pronounce a title More hateful to mine ear.
MACBETH	No, nor more fearful.
Y. SIWARD	Thou liest, abhorred tyrant, with my sword 10 I'll prove the lie thou speak'st.

[*They fight, and* YOUNG SIWARD *is slain*

MACBETH	Thou wast born of woman. But swords I smile at, weapons laugh to scorn, Brandished by man that's of a woman born. [*Exit*

Alarums. Enter MACDUFF

MACDUFF	That way the noise is. Tyrant, show thy face.
	If thou be'st slain, and with no stroke of mine,
	My wife and children's ghosts will haunt me still.
	I cannot strike at wretched kerns, whose arms
	Are hired to bear their staves. Either thou,
	   Macbeth,
	Or else my sword, with an unbattered edge
	I sheath again undeeded. There thou shouldst
	   be; 20
	By this great clatter, one of greatest note
	Seems bruited. Let me find him, fortune,
	And more I beg not. [*Exit. Alarums*

Enter MALCOLM *and* SIWARD

SIWARD	This way my lord, the castle's gently rendered. The tyrant's people on both sides do fight; The noble thanes do bravely in the war; The day almost itself professes yours,

We have...beside us: our enemies have been fighting on our side/our enemies have deliberately aimed to miss us with their swords

Macduff catches up with Macbeth. They begin to fight, but Macbeth tells Macduff that he is wasting his time because no man born of woman can hurt him. Macduff says that he was born by a Caesarean operation.

Roman fool: (defeated Roman soldiers committed suicide rather than suffer the humiliation of capture)
lives: enemies alive
Of all men else: more than all other men
charged: burdened
terms: words
Thou...labour: you are tiring
intrenchant: uncuttable, that cannot be hurt
vulnerable crests: heads that can be wounded
must not: cannot
Despair thy charm: lose all trust in your charm
angel...served: evil angel you have always served
Untimely: before time, prematurely (Macduff was delivered by a Caesarean section, and could therefore be said not to have been 'born'.)

And little is to do.

MALCOLM   We have met with foes
That strike beside us.

SIWARD   Enter, sir, the castle.
                                             [*Exeunt. Alarum*

Scene 8

The battleground before the castle

Enter MACBETH

MACBETH   Why should I play the Roman fool, and die
            On mine own sword? Whiles I see lives, the gashes
            Do better upon them.

Enter MACDUFF

MACDUFF   Turn hell-hound, turn!

MACBETH   Of all men else I have avoided thee.
            But get thee back, my soul is too much charged
            With blood of thine already.

MACDUFF   I have no words:
            My voice is in my sword, thou bloodier villain
            Than terms can give thee out!   [*They fight*

MACBETH   Thou losest labour;
            As easy mayst thou the intrenchant air
            With thy keen sword impress, as make me
                bleed.   10
            Let fall thy blade on vulnerable crests;
            I bear a charmed life, which must not yield
            To one of woman born.

MACDUFF   Despair thy charm,
            And let the angel whom thou still hast served
            Tell thee, Macduff was from his mother's womb
            Untimely ripped.

Macbeth is totally disheartened and refuses to fight on.
Macduff says Macbeth will be taken around the
countryside like a fairground freak. At this threat,
Macbeth fights and is killed.

---

cowed my...man: intimidated my manly spirit (made me a
  coward)
juggling: cheating (juggling with words)
palter: equivocate
break it...hope: dash our hopes
show and...time: spectacle of our age
monsters: freaks
Painted...underwrit: advertised by a painting on a pole, with
  this caption
rabble: commoners
opposed: in opposition
I will try the last: I will fight to the end
Lay on: fight on
Exeunt, fighting/Enter fighting: Many of Shakespeare's
  audience were practised swordsmen and would appreciate a
  good stage fight. Macbeth and Macduff leave the stage
  fighting, continue – by means of sound effects – offstage,
  and re-enter, usually on another part of the stage, still
  fighting. Macbeth's body is removed by soldiers.

The victorious army are counting their losses.

---

we miss: who are missing
go off: be killed
by these: judging by these already here

MACBETH   Accursed be that tongue that tells me so,
           For it hath cowed my better part of man.
           And be these juggling fiends no more believed,
           That palter with us in a double sense;   20
           That keep the word of promise to our ear,
           And break it to our hope. I'll not fight with thee.

MACDUFF   Then yield thee, coward,
           And live to be the show and gaze o' th' time.
           We'll have thee, as our rarer monsters are,
           Painted upon a pole, and underwrit,
           'Here may you see the tyrant.'

MACBETH   I will not yield,
           To kiss the ground before young Malcolm's feet,
           And to be baited with the rabble's curse.
           Though Birnam wood be come to Dunsinane,   30
           And thou opposed, being of no woman born,
           Yet I will try the last. Before my body
           I throw my warlike shield. Lay on Macduff,
           And damned to him that first cries 'Hold, enough!'
                            [*Exeunt, fighting. Alarums*

           Enter fighting and MACBETH *slain*

Scene

Courtyard of the castle

Retreat. Flourish. Enter, with drum and colours,
MALCOLM, SIWARD, ROSS, LENNOX, ANGUS,
CAITHNESS, MENTEITH, *and* SOLDIERS

MALCOLM   I would the friends we miss were safe arrived.

SIWARD   Some must go off; and yet by these I see,
           So great a day as this is cheaply bought.

MALCOLM   Macduff is missing, and your noble son.

Siward learns of his son's death, and refuses to mourn for him because he did his duty and so is in God's care. Macduff brings in Macbeth's head on a stake. Malcolm promises to reward all those who deserve it.

paid a soldier's debt: been killed

prowess: bravery

In the...fought: in the post where he fought without flinching

before: in front (i.e. he was not struck in the back, running away)

hairs: (play on words – *hairs/heirs*)

knolled: tolled (his death-bell is rung, there is no more to be said)

parted well...score: died bravely and did his duty

newer comfort: more good news

The time is free: this age has recovered its freedom

compassed...pearl: surrounded by the jewels (most worthy people) of your country – like pearls around a crown

salutation: greeting as a salute to you

spend...time: we shall not be long

reckon...loves: reward the love/loyalty of each of you

make us...you: pay our debts to you

ROSS	Your son, my lord, has paid a soldier's debt:
	He only lived but till he was a man,
	The which no sooner had his prowess confirmed
	In the unshrinking station where he fought,
	But like a man he died.
SIWARD	Then he is dead?
ROSS	Ay, and brought off the field. Your cause of
	sorrow 10
	Must not be measured by his worth, for then
	It hath no end.
SIWARD	Had he his hurts before?
ROSS	Ay, on the front.
SIWARD	Why then, God's soldier be he.
	Had I as many sons as I have hairs,
	I would not wish them to a fairer death.
	And so, his knell is knolled.
MALCOLM	He's worth more sorrow,
	And that I'll spend for him.
SIWARD	He's worth no more.
	They say he parted well, and paid his score.
	And so God be with him. Here comes newer
	comfort.

Re-enter MACDUFF, *with* MACBETH'S *head*

MACDUFF	Hail, King, for so thou art. Behold where stands 20
	Th' usurper's cursed head. The time is free.
	I see thee compassed with thy kingdom's pearl,
	That speak my salutation in their minds;
	Whose voices I desire aloud with mine:
	Hail, King of Scotland!
ALL	Hail, King of Scotland! [*Flourish*
MALCOLM	We shall not spend a large expense of time,
	Before we reckon with your several loves,
	And make us even with you. My thanes and
	kinsmen,

Malcolm intends to hunt down all those who committed atrocities for Macbeth. He says it is thought that Lady Macbeth committed suicide. He invites all present to his coronation.

In such...named: named with this honourable title
planted newly...time: established at the beginning of this new age (horticultural imagery; see Act 1 scene 4 lines 28–29)
snares: means of being trapped
watchful: with spies
Producing forth: seeking out
ministers: those acting for
by self and: by her own
Grace: God
in measure: appropriately, in due proportion

ACTIVITIES

Keeping track

Scene 4

1 What is the connection between the Third Apparition and Malcolm's army?

Scene 5

2 What is Macbeth's reaction to the news of Lady Macbeth's death?

3 What makes Macbeth decide that he has nothing to lose by attacking the enemy?

Scene 7

4 Who does Macbeth kill in battle?

Henceforth be earls, the first that ever Scotland
In such an honour named. What's more to do,   30
Which would be planted newly with the time –
As calling home our exiled friends abroad,
That fled the snares of watchful tyranny,
Producing forth the cruel ministers
Of this dead butcher, and his fiend-like queen,
Who as 'tis thought, by self and violent hands
Took off her life – this, and what needful else
That calls upon us, by the grace of Grace,
We will perform in measure, time and place.
So thanks to all at once, and to each one,   40
Whom we invite to see us crowned at Scone.

[*Flourish. Exeunt*

Scene 8

5 How does Macduff 'fit' the message of the Second Apparition?

Scene 9

6 How is the warning of the First Apparition fulfilled?

Discussion

1 '*She should have died hereafter;*
   There would have been a time for such a word'
   Can you explain Macbeth's reaction to the news of Lady
   Macbeth's death? Is he unfeeling? Is he too full of emotion to
   express himself? Are there other reasons for his response?
2 What do you feel that Macbeth is thinking at these key
   moments:
   • scene 5 lines 1–7
   • scene 5 lines 33–35

- scene 7 lines 11–13
- scene 8 lines 1–3
- scene 8 lines 14–17
- scene 8 lines 23–27 ?

3 How would you describe Old Siward's reaction to his son's death? What are we supposed to think of Old Siward? Is that what we really think about him?

Drama

1 After his coronation Malcolm commissions a tapestry – like the Bayeux tapestry – depicting the Battle of Dunsinane. Imagine that you have been asked to submit a design. Using the text and the stories told by soldiers, create a section of this tapestry. Work in groups of five or six. Use still image techniques (see FREEZE! page 227.)

2 Look at the speech 'She should have died hereafter...Signifying nothing', (scene 5 lines 17–28).

- Divide each line up into syllables and count them. What is the pattern? Where are the irregularities, and what is the reason for them? Why has the last line only six syllables? (Try breathing out for four beats.)
- Learn the whole speech.
- The whole class can practise it together. Experiment with the volume and tone. Try decreasing the number of speakers until the final word is spoken by one person. People often find that they get a 'feel' for the language of a play when they speak, rather than just read, the lines.
- Has this speech had any effect on you? Did you find any interesting sounds? Are there any words, phrases or images which made an impression on you? Do you think you understand the character of Macbeth better for having read his lines?

Character

1 a Macbeth's evil actions result, justly you might think, in his death. But are there any occasions in the later stages

of the play when you feel sympathy for him? Is there a time, perhaps, when you even admire him? Why is this? Do we see a side of his character which has not been evident before – or, at least, not for a long time?

b From scene 4 there is a great deal of 'manly' talk about fighting by Malcolm's forces. Whose attitude to war, and the language he uses, is most like that of Macbeth? Explain why you think this might be.

2 *Re-enter* MACDUFF, *with* MACBETH's *head*
What are Macduff's feelings at this time? Bear in mind what he has said previously, especially on these occasions:
• Act 4 scene 3 lines 230–235
• Act 5 scene 7 lines 14–20
• Act 5 scene 8 lines 6–8
• Act 5 scene 8 lines 23–27

3 Bring your CHARACTER LOGS to a close.

Close study

1 a The notes for scene 5 lines 19–28, tell us that there are five different images in these lines.
   • Write out Macbeth's speech.
   • Using a different colour for each image, underline the words and phrases which refer to sound, movement, time, light and the theatre.

b In the same speech, why does the reference to '*brief candle*' remind us of Act 5 scene 1? In what other ways does this speech echo the actions and words of the earlier scene?

2 Macduff represents Macbeth's fate or nemesis, his reward for evil.

   Look at how Shakespeare has structured Act 5 to bring them together in scene 8.

   Make two lists of the first seven scenes:
   • one for scenes 1, 3, 5 and 7
   • the other for scenes 2, 4, 6 and 7.
   Alongside each list have two columns, one for the main character/s involved in that scene, and the other for the number of lines in the scene.

In the diagram the lists have been started for you:

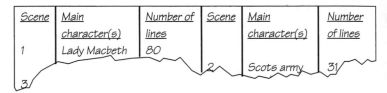

Scene	Main character(s)	Number of lines	Scene	Main character(s)	Number of lines
1	Lady Macbeth	80			
			2	Scots army	31
3					

Scene 7 is on both lists because Macbeth and Macduff are involved separately. Work out how many lines are devoted to each character within that scene.

- Why are the scenes arranged alternately in this way?
- Why do the scenes become shorter and shorter?
- What was Shakespeare's intention? Has he been successful?

3 From the end of Act 3 onwards other characters speak of Macbeth in the most unflattering terms. Find these descriptions of him (and their speakers) and list them in an 'Insults chart', starting with the most insulting description at the top and working down to the least insulting – but still quite offensive! Compare your chart with the charts of others in the group.

Writing

1 **Malcolm, King of Scotland**

From the evidence of your CHARACTER LOG of Malcolm, and particularly from his speech at the end of the play, what sort of king do you think Malcolm will prove to be? (For help with organizing this work, see WRITING ABOUT CHARACTER, page 234.)

2 In medieval times a popular form of story-telling was the ballad. Ballads were verses set to music, and they were about well-known people or events. Often the verses were four lines long, and the second and fourth lines rhymed. Sometimes they would have a chorus, perhaps of two lines, repeated at regular intervals – not necessarily after every verse.

Write the Ballad of Macbeth (with or without a chorus),
covering the main events of the play.

3 Write an obituary for Macbeth, in which you try to emphasize
his good points.

Quiz

Who said the following, and to whom?

1 'The Queen, my lord, is dead'

2 'The devil himself could not pronounce a title
More hateful to mine ear'

3 'my soul is too much charged
With blood of thine already'

Who said the following, and about whom?

4 'And none serve him but constrained things,
Whose hearts are absent too'

5 'And be these juggling fiends no more believed,
That palter with us in a double sense'

6 'Your son my lord, has paid a soldier's debt:
He only lived but till he was a man'

Who said the following, when, and about what?

7 'Within this three mile may you see it coming.
I say, a moving grove'

8 'Macduff was from his mother's womb
Untimely ripped'

9 'Behold where stands
Th' usurper's cursed head'

Who said the following, when, and about what? Comment on
the imagery.

10 'They have tied me to a stake; I cannot fly,
But bear-like I must fight the course'

The plot at a glance

1i	The three witches	Influence of supernatural
1ii	The captain's report	Macbeth's reputation
1iii	The prophecies	Macbeth's ambition stirred
1iv	Duncan's gratitude	Malcolm heir to throne
1v	Macbeth's letter	Lady Macbeth's reaction
1vi	Duncan visits Macbeth	Dramatic irony of situation
1vii	Macbeth hesitates	Lady Macbeth's scorn
2i	'Is this a dagger...?'	Macbeth troubled
2ii	Duncan's murder	Macbeth's conscience
2iii	Body discovered	The Macbeths are defensive
2iv	Ross and the old man	Natural world in disorder
3i	Murderers hired	Attempt to defy prophecy
3ii	Lady Macbeth not told	Macbeth continues evil course
3iii	Banquo's murder	Escape of Fleance
3iv	Banquo's ghost	Strain is showing
3v	Hecate and the witches	Reinforcement of supernatural
3vi	Lennox and a lord	Suspicions about Macbeth
4i	The apparitions	Macbeth given encouragement
4ii	Macduff family killed	Height of Macbeth's evil
4iii	Macduff sees Malcolm	Macbeth's opponents organized
5i	Sleepwalking scene	Lady Macbeth's deterioration
5ii	Scottish soldiers	Opposition to Macbeth grows
5iii	Macbeth at Dunsinane	Macbeth confident but frantic
5iv	Malcolm at Birnam Wood	Equivocation of Apparition 3
5v	Lady Macbeth's death	'Moving wood' daunts Macbeth
5vi	Malcolm ready to fight	Macbeth almost alone
5vii	Death of Young Siward	Macduff stalks Macbeth
5viii	Death of Macbeth	Equivocation of Apparition 2
5ix	Malcolm declared king	Fulfilment of Apparition 1

Macbeth has won two great victories. The witches prophesy that he will be king; and that Banquo will be the ancestor of kings. When Duncan names Malcolm as his successor, Macbeth begins to contemplate murder. Lady Macbeth, inspired by Macbeth's letter, is determined to help him become king. Duncan stays with them overnight and she persuades Macbeth to go ahead with plans for Duncan's murder.

Macbeth kills Duncan and is shaken by what he has done. The guards are suspected of being involved, but Macbeth has killed them too. Duncan's sons, Malcolm and Donalbain fear for their lives and flee.

Aware of the witches' prophecy to Banquo, Macbeth hires two murderers. They kill Banquo, but Fleance escapes. Banquo's ghost appears to Macbeth at the banquet, and Macbeth is distraught. Lady Macbeth asks the guests to leave. Macbeth is angry that Macduff is avoiding him. He decides to visit the witches again to find out what the future holds.

The apparitions apparently give Macbeth comforting news, but the show of kings displeases him. Macbeth orders the deaths of Macduff's family. Malcolm has an army to oppose Macbeth.

Lady Macbeth is breaking down under the strain of recent events. Macbeth, deserted by most of his followers, is also becoming frenzied. Malcolm's English army is reinforced by many Scots who want to see the end of Macbeth. Lady Macbeth dies. The battle of Dunsinane is quickly over. Macbeth is killed by Macduff and Malcolm is named king.

Explorations

Keeping track

When you are studying a play one of the most difficult things to do is to keep track of all the ideas and information you gain as you work on it scene by scene. It is important to keep a note of what you do. Two good ways of organizing your work are to keep a SCENE LOG and a CHARACTER LOG.

Scene log

As you work on each scene, make a list of the basic information about it:
- when and where it takes place
- the characters in it
- what happens.

Then add any thoughts and comments you want to remember. You could use the layout illustrated opposite – or you may prefer to make up your own.

Character log

At the same time, you can keep a log for each of the main characters. Use this to record what you find out about the character in every scene s/he appears in:
- key points about the character
- your reasons for choosing these
- the numbers of important lines
- short quotations to back up the key points.

Again, there is a layout opposite, but you may prefer your own approach.

Scene log

Act/scene	Time/place	Characters	Action	Comments
1/2	Day, the same	Duncan, Malcolm, Captain	It is reported that Macbeth has led the Scottish army to two great victories in one day. The Thane of Cawdor is a traitor. His title will go to Macbeth.	Macbeth is established as a heroic figure; a contrast to King Duncan.

Character log

Character: Macbeth

Act/scene	Key points	Reasons	Key lines	Short quotations
1/2	Heroic fighter	Scornful of Macdonwald and his army	16–23	brave Macbeth – well he deserves that name
	Heroic attitude	Fearlessly faces the fresh Norwegian army	33–38	

Character activities

Quotations

When talking or writing about a character, it is important to be able to back up what you say by referring to the play. You could say, 'I know this is true of this character because in Act 1 scene 2 he says this, or does that!' You should have lots of information for the main characters in your CHARACTER LOGS. It is useful to have some of it in your head. A good way of remembering is to have a 'nutshell' quotation for each character – a few words which really sum up the character, or describe him/her 'in a nutshell'. For instance, you might think of Macbeth as 'Bellona's bridegroom' or 'full o' th' milk of human kindness' or 'abhorred tyrant'. Which do you think is the most fitting description?

1 For each of the main characters find two or three 'nutshell' quotations. They may be the character's own words, or something said by another character about him/her.

2 Go through your list and choose the best one for each character.

3 Work in a group and try out your quotations on the others. Make a group list of the best 'nutshell' quotation for each character.

Who's who?

On page 81 (CHARACTER 1) you cast a modern day actor/character to play the part of the porter.

1 Bearing in mind their characters, which other actors do you think would be most suitable to play the following roles:
- Macbeth
- Lady Macbeth
- the three witches
- Duncan
- Banquo
- Macduff
- Lady Macduff

- Lady Macduff's son
- Malcolm
- the two murderers ?

2 Given this 'all-star' cast, which of your school friends could best fill the other parts?

Secret files

In any play, the writer presents us with key moments in the lives of the characters and leaves us to work out the rest for ourselves. It is interesting to ask questions about those parts of the characters' lives that the writer does not tell us about. For example:

- Was Duncan ever a forceful king?
- How did Lady Macbeth meet Macbeth?
- What is Macbeth's military history?

1 Choose one of the main characters.

2 Make up a list of questions about that character that you would like answered.

3 Build up a complete 'secret file' about your chosen character. Start with the character's childhood and go on adding information up to the end of the play, or up to the character's death. You can make up as much as you like, provided nothing contradicts the facts of the play and the behaviour of your character in it.

4 Compare your 'secret file' with that of at least one other person who has been working on the same character. Are the additional 'facts' interesting? Are they believable? If you were to do this work again, what alterations would you make in **2**, above?

Arrows of influence

The purpose of this activity is to clarify how the characters inter-act; that is, how much one character influences another, or others. (The influence might be good or bad.) Influence is shown by arrows: the direction of the arrow shows who is influencing whom; the stronger the influence, the thicker the arrow. For example:

With Macbeth in the centre of your diagram and the other characters around the edges, show the arrows of influence.

Chain of events

This is the story of *Macbeth* in the form of a diagram. This time the arrows are of uniform thickness. Can you explain what event in the play each numbered arrow represents?

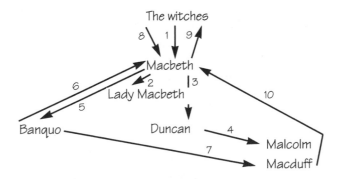

Contrasts

A playwright will often emphasize a feature of one character by contrasting him/her with another character in the same – or a similar – situation.

What contrasts does Shakespeare point out in the following:

- Duncan/Macbeth and Banquo as soldiers
- Macbeth/Banquo in their reaction to the witches
- Macbeth/Banquo after consideration of the prophecies
- Macbeth/Lady Macbeth in their reaction to Duncan's murder
- Macbeth/Macduff in their reaction to the discovery of Duncan's body
- Macbeth/Macduff in their attitude to the other's wife
- Macbeth/Macduff in their reaction to the death of their own wife
- Macbeth/Duncan as king

Innermost thoughts

Through their soliloquies we learn what characters are really thinking. At other times, perhaps, we can guess what a character is thinking, and it might be quite different from what s/he says. What are the character's innermost thoughts when these words are spoken?

- 'My hands are of your colour; but I shame
  To wear a heart so white.'
  Act 2 scene 2 lines 61–62
- 'Tonight we hold a solemn supper, sir,
  And I'll request your presence.'
  Act 3 scene 1 lines 14–15
- 'Sit, worthy friends. My lord is often thus,
  And hath been from his youth.'
  Act 3 scene 4 lines 53–54
- 'But fear not yet
  To take upon you what is yours.'
  Act 4 scene 3 lines 69–70
- 'Were I from Dunsinane away, and clear,
  Profit again should hardly draw me here.'
  Act 5 scene 3 lines 61–62

Themes

Elements of the supernatural

The witches	Act 1 Scene 3	seen by Macbeth, Banquo
The dagger	Act 2 Scene 1	seen by Macbeth
Banquo's ghost	Act 3 Scene 4	seen by Macbeth
The apparitions	Act 4 Scene 1	seen by Macbeth

1 What is the different effect on Macbeth's life of:
   - the prophecies of the witches
   - the apparitions?
2 What is the connection between Macbeth, Banquo's ghost and the witches?
3 How are the words of the apparitions fulfilled?
4 Some people say that the witches must be real because Banquo sees them. Others argue that they are unreal, and that they represent Macbeth's evil ambitions. They say that Macbeth 'sees' the dagger and Banquo's ghost, and so it is reasonable to assume that the witches are also products of his disturbed mind. According to this theory, Banquo sees the witches because, at the time, he has unworthy ambitions, too.

   What do you think: are the witches real or not?

Evil

These notes are one way of tracing the path of evil through the play. Why do you think each note has been included? What else would you add?
- 'Fair is foul' (Act 1 scene 1)
- Act 1 scene 3 lines 134–137
- 'Prince of Cumberland' (Act 1 scene 4)
- 'The raven himself is hoarse' (Act 1 scene 5)
- 'Is this a dagger?...Tarquin...' (Act 2 scene 1)
- 'could not say "Amen"' (Act 2 scene 2)
- Act 3 scene 1 lines 75–142

- '*Be innocent of the knowledge, dearest chuck*' (Act 3 scene 2)
- '*I am in blood Stepped in so far...*' (Act 3 scene 4)
- '*How now, you...hags!*' [attitude!] (Act 4 scene 1)
- '*...Even till destruction sicken*' (Act 4 scene 1)
- Act 4 scene 1 lines 149–153; Act 4 scene 2
- Act 5 scene 1 (sleepwalkers doomed to damnation)

Nemesis

Nemesis was the goddess of retribution, or vengeance. The word 'nemesis' is often used, therefore, to represent retribution.

It can be said that as soon as Macbeth and Lady Macbeth began their life of evil, their fate was sealed: they would get what they deserved; it was only a matter of time. We know that they did get what they deserved, and we also know it did not happen all at once, but in stages.

Ten stages are listed below, but not in the order in which they happen. What is the correct order?

- The Thanes' desertion of Macbeth
- Lady Macbeth's unease after becoming queen
- The decision to 'surprise' Macduff's castle
- The apparitions' equivocation
- Lady Macbeth's madness and death
- Macbeth's inability to say 'Amen'
- Macbeth's unease after becoming king
- The appearance of Banquo's ghost
- Macbeth's death
- Disturbed sleep

Ambition

1 Who says the following, about whom or what, and when?
- '*Good sir, why do you start, and seem to fear
Things that do sound so fair?*'
- '*Two truths are told
As happy prologues to the swelling act
Of the imperial theme.*'

- '*The Prince of Cumberland – that is a step,*
  On which I must fall down, or else o'erleap,
  For in my way it lies.'
- '*Thou wouldst be great,*
  Art not without ambition, but without
  The illness should attend it.'
- '*I have no spur*
  To prick the sides of my intent, but only
  Vaulting ambition'

2 At the beginning of the play Macbeth is co-leader of the
   Scottish army, and Thane of Glamis. During the course of
   the play he is known by other titles – and names! – which
   trace the course of his ambition. Make a list of them.

3 Do you think Macbeth was ambitious to become king from
   the very beginning of the play, or does his ambition grow
   only from the moment he hears the prophecies? How far is
   his ambition spurred by Lady Macbeth?

Sleep and darkness/Night

There are a number of references, especially early in the play,
to both sleep and darkness (or blackness or night). These
references are given in the order in which they occur in the
play. Sort them out into two separate lists, one for Sleep and
one for Darkness.

Act 1 scene 3 lines 19–20
Act 1 scene 4 lines 50–53
Act 1 scene 5 lines 50–54
Act 2 scene 1 lines 4–5, 7, 50–51
Act 2 scene 2 lines 32–37, 37–40
Act 2 scene 3 line 74
Act 2 scene 4 lines 6–10
Act 3 scene 2 lines 17–19, 23, 46–53
Act 3 scene 4 line 141

It could be said that one list is mainly concerned with evil, and
the other with nemesis. Which is which?

Love

1 'LADY MACBETH: *Great Glamis, worthy Cawdor...*
  MACBETH: *My dearest love...*'
  These are the words with which Macbeth and Lady Macbeth
  greet each other at their first meeting in the play. By the time
  of Lady Macbeth's death they are saying very little to each
  other. Some think that their relationship changes with the
  death of Duncan.
    Look again at their conversations from Act 2 scene 2
  onwards. Do you think that there is a change in the
  relationship? If so, can you explain why this might be?

2 Is Shakespeare's portrayal of Lady Macduff and her son a good
  example of family love? What leads you to this opinion?

Loyalty

Although the main thread of the play is concerned with treachery,
there are, nevertheless, examples of loyalty. Unfortunately, we see
that loyalty can have bitter rewards.

1 What example of loyalty is seen in Act 3 scene 1 lines 1–3?
  Why do you think that character chooses to be loyal? What is
  the character's reward for loyalty?

2 To whom or what does a character show loyalty in Act 4 scene
  3 lines 31–33 and 100? In pursuing this particular loyalty the
  character has also been disloyal on a personal level, with tragic
  consequences. Explain this. How is the loyalty eventually
  rewarded?

Courage

There are numerous examples of physical courage in this play,
from the reports of Macbeth's prowess in battle in Act 1 to his
insistence on fighting Macduff to the death (although he knows
from the apparitions that he cannot win) in Act 5. They include
the captain's report to Duncan whilst severely wounded and
Young Siward's challenge to Macbeth in battle.
  The most remarkable instance of courage, however, is

Macduff's open opposition to Macbeth after the death of Duncan. Find quotations from Act 2 scene 3 onwards which trace this opposition. Your quotations should tell a story in miniature, perhaps beginning with '*Wherefore did you so?*'(Act 2 scene 3 line 105) which shows Macduff's first suspicions, and ending with '*Behold, where stands the usurper's cursed head*'.

Order and disorder

Shakespeare's Jacobean audiences believed that things in the universe were part of a divine order and that all things were linked together in a great chain of being. Kings had a divine right to rule, given by God and, as all parts of creation were linked together, any threat to the king would also be a threat to the natural order of society and would bring chaos to the heavens. The overturning of natural order is heralded in the witches' '*Fair is foul, and foul is fair*' in Act 1 scene 1. In the course of the play, just as Macbeth's '*single state of man*' becomes confused (and '*nothing is But what is not*'), so the natural order of things descends into chaos.

Find other references in the play to the overturning of the natural order.

Shakespeare's language

It is easy to look at the text of this play and say to yourself, 'I'm never going to understand that!' But it is important not to be put off. Remember that there are two reasons why Shakespeare's language may seem strange at first:

1 He was writing 400 years ago and the English language has changed over the centuries.

2 He wrote mainly in verse. As a result he sometimes changed the order of words to make them fit the verse form, and he used a large number of 'tricks of the trade': figures of speech and other verse techniques (which are listed in the GLOSSARY, page 238).

Language change

This can cause three main kinds of problem:

Grammar

Since the end of the sixteenth century, there have been some changes in English grammar. Some examples:

1 *Thee, thou, thy,* and the verb forms that go with them:
   '*This have I thought good to deliver thee, my dearest partner of greatness, that thou mightest not lose the dues of rejoicing, by being ignorant of what greatness is promised thee. Lay it to thy heart, and farewell.*'

2 Words contract (shorten) in different ways. For example:
   'tis rather than *it's*
   who is't for *who is it*

3 Some of the 'little words' are different. For example: *an* for *if*

Words that have changed their meaning

Sometimes you will come across words that you think you know, but discover that they don't mean what you expect them to mean. For example:
   today *presently* means *in a while,* but in Act 1 scene 2 line 64 *present* means *immediate*

would can also have the meaning of *wish* or *want* ('*Would they had stayed!*' Act 1 scene 3 line 82)

Words that have gone out of use

These are the most obvious and most frequent causes of difficulty. You can work out the meaning of some of them (*faith-breach, here-approach*) but others will be totally unfamiliar to you (*aroint, avaunt*).

Shakespeare had – and used – a huge vocabulary. He loved using words, and pushing them to their limits. So you will come across many words you have not met before. They are usually explained in the notes.

The language of the play

Most of *Macbeth* is in *blank verse*, but parts are in *prose* and some sections are in *rhymed verse*.

Blank verse

The main part of the play is written in lines of ten syllables, with a repeated even pattern of weak and strong 'beats':

'*What **bloody man** is **that** he **can report**'*

(ti **tum** ti **tum** ti **tum** ti **tum** ti **tum**)

If Shakespeare had made every line exactly the same, the play would soon become very monotonous, so he varies the rhythm in a number of ways. Often he just changes the pattern of weak and strong slightly:

'*What **he** hath **lost**, **noble** Mac**beth** hath **won**'*

(ti **tum** ti **tum** **tum** ti ti **tum** ti **tum**)

On occasions the rhythm is changed by adding an extra syllable:

'*But / the / Nor/wey/an / lord, / sur/vey/ing / van/tage*'

Sometimes there will be fewer syllables, for effect:

'*Or memorize another Golgotha*
I / can/not / tell –'

Shakespeare also writes so that sentences sometimes finish at the end of a line, and at other times in the middle:

> *'Shall not be long but I'll be here again.*
> *Things at the worst will cease, or else climb upward*
> *To what they were before.'*

So the verse of the play has a strong but varied rhythm. Most of the lines do not rhyme, so they are 'blank' – hence the term *blank verse*.

Rhymed verse

Sometimes Shakespeare uses a pattern of rhymed lines. It may be just two successive lines (a *rhyming couplet*), often rounding off a scene:

> *'Away, and mock the time with fairest show:*
> *False face must hide what the false heart doth know;'*

or it might be a rhyming couplet or two to emphasize a decision or a sense of purpose:

> *'Stars hide your fires,*
> *Let not light see my black and deep desires.*
> *The eye wink at the hand; yet let that be,*
> *Which the eye fears when it is done to see.'*

The witches speak mainly in couplets, but, to show that they are not human, they use a different rhythm and fewer syllables:

> *'**Though** his **bark** cannot be **lost**,*
> ***Yet** it **shall** be tempest-**tossed**.'*

Prose

In some scenes, characters' speeches are not written in blank or rhymed verse, but in 'ordinary sentences' – prose. If you look at the play as a whole, you will see that prose is used for certain characters and situations. Look, for example, at these sections:

> Act 2 scene 3 lines 1–40
> Act 5 scene 1 lines 1–70.

Can you work out why prose is used in each case?

Drama activities

Most of these activities can be done in small groups or by the class as a whole. They work by slowing down the action of the play and helping you focus on a small section of it – so that you can think more deeply about characters, plot and themes.

Hotseating

Hotseating means putting one of the characters 'under the microscope' at a particular point in the play. This is how it works:

1 Begin by choosing a particular character and a particular moment in the play. For example, you might choose Macbeth after the murder of Macduff's family.
2 One person (student or teacher) is selected to be the chosen character.
3 That person sits 'in the hotseat', with the rest of the group arranged round in a semi-circle, or a circle.
4 The rest then ask questions about how the character feels, why s/he has acted in that way, and so on. Try to keep the questions going and not to give the person in the hotseat too much time to think.

Variations

1 The questioners themselves take on roles. (In the example above they could be Macduff, Ross, Malcolm, and even Lady Macduff.)
2 Characters can be hotseated at a series of key moments in a scene to see how their opinions and attitudes change.
3 The questioners can take different attitudes to the character, for example:
 • aggressive
 • pleading
 • disbelieving.

Freeze!

It is very useful to be able to 'stop the action' and concentrate on a single moment in the play. You can do this in a number of ways.

Photographs

Imagine that someone has taken a photograph of a particular moment, or that – as if it were a film or video – the action has been frozen. Once you have chosen the moment, you can work in a number of different ways:

- Act that part of the scene and then 'Freeze!' – you will probably find it easier if you have a 'director' standing outside the scene to shout 'Freeze!'
- Discuss what the photograph should look like and then arrange yourselves into the photograph.
- One at a time place yourselves in the photograph; each person 'entering' it must take notice of what is there already.
- Once you have arranged the photograph, take it in turns to come out of it and comment on it, with suggestions for improvements.

There are a number of ways in which you can develop your photograph:

- Each person takes it in turn to speak his/her thoughts at that moment in the scene.
- The photograph is given a caption.
- Some members of the group do not take part in the photograph. Instead they provide a sound track of speech or sound effects, or both.

Statues/Paintings

Make a statue or a painting like this:

1 Select a moment in the play, or a title from the play (for example, 'All hail, Macbeth')
2 Choose one member of the group to be the sculptor/painter. That person then arranges the rest of the group, one at a time, to make the statue or painting. Statues and paintings are different from photographs in two important ways:

- they are made up by an 'artist' and tell us about the artist's view of the person or event;
- if they talk, they tell us about what they can 'see', for example, how people react when they see the statue or painting for the first time.

Forum theatre

In FORUM THEATRE, one or two people take on roles and the rest of the group are 'directors'. It works like this:

1 Select a moment in the play. (For example, the moment when Macbeth is told Birnam Wood is moving.)
2 Select a member of the group to be Macbeth.
3 Organize your working area, so that everyone knows where the other characters are, where characters make entrances and exits, and so on.
4 Begin by asking Macbeth to offer his own first thoughts about position, gesture, and movement.
5 The directors then experiment with different ways of presenting that moment. They can:
  - ask Macbeth to take up a particular position, use a particular gesture, move in a certain way
  - ask him to speak in a particular way
  - discuss with Macbeth how he might move or speak and why – for example, to communicate a certain set of thoughts and feelings.
6 The short sequence can be repeated a number of times, until the directors have used up all their ideas about their interpretation.

Talk it over: ideas for discussion

These discussions will be most effective if held with groups of three or four. When you have had time to exchange ideas and come to some conclusions, share your thoughts with others in the class. Sometimes this 'reporting back' will involve the whole class; sometimes it will mean comparing notes with one other group. On occasions, the original groups can be split and new groupings made, with each member bringing the thoughts and suggestions from their first group.

1   Look closely at the scenes involving the witches, especially Act 1 scene 3 and Act 4 scene 1. In what ways does Shakespeare show that three and multiples of three are magic/mystic numbers?

2   Some people feel that Macbeth is bewitched before the play begins, because he is under the influence of his wife. They point to Lady Macbeth's response to Macbeth's letter in Act 1 scene 5 and her call upon the evil spirits to help her. They argue that such an instant reaction would only come from a person involved with the supernatural. Others say that the end of the play makes nonsense of this idea. What do you think?

3   In Act 2 scene 1 lines 33–61 Macbeth is obviously still uneasy about committing the murder of Duncan. When you consider his character up to this point in the play, and the reasons he gave in Act 1 scene 7 for not killing Duncan, this is understandable. Although he has time to change his mind, he goes through with the murder. Why does he do it? Is it perhaps a sign of a weakness in his character?

4   In Act 3 scene 1 a servant brings the murderers to Macbeth. Macbeth confesses to the murderers that Banquo is his enemy before they have agreed to kill him. Things are spoken in front of servants as if they do not exist. From these incidents, what would you say was the place of the common man in eleventh-century Scottish society?

5   On pages 122 and 123 (DISCUSSION and DRAMA) you looked at the two entrances of Banquo's ghost. Look again at Act 3 scene 4. Take note of what Macbeth says shortly before and

after each entrance. If you were directing the play, would you change the ghost's entrances to fit more dramatically with what Macbeth is saying? If so, after what lines would you have the ghost enter?

6 Ross is agitated in Act 4 scene 2 and promises to return to see how Lady Macduff is. We know that Lady Macduff is threatened. Why, then, does Shakespeare include a messenger in this scene? What is the dramatic purpose of lines 63–71?

7 In Act 4 scene 3 why does it seem to take so long for Macduff to absorb the news of his family's deaths? What are the many thoughts that must be going through his mind from his first suspicions of bad news (line 180) to the end of the scene?

8 Nothing is resolved at the end of the sleepwalking scene; so:
  • why did the gentlewoman call in the doctor?
  • what did she expect him to do?
  • why does the doctor say, '*I think, but I dare not speak*'?
  • to whom could he report?
  • what could he say?
  • what would be the result of that?

9 In Act 5 scene 5 how would you say Macbeth's mood changes in the following sections of the scene: lines 1–7; lines 9–15; lines 17–28; line 35; lines 38–40; lines 40–46; lines 46–52?

10 Go through the play and say briefly when each scene takes place. Start with Act 1 scene 1 as Day 1. Is Act 1 scene 2 at the same time, later the same day or next day, for instance?

Writing activities

Imaginative writing

1 **The Macduff letters**
When Macduff left for England he obviously did so without discussing his action with his wife. Imagine **either** that Macduff left an undiscovered letter to Lady Macduff, in which he explains his reasons for leaving Scotland; **or** that Lady Macduff wrote a letter to her husband before her death, expressing her feelings about him. Write one of these letters.

2 **Don't shoot the messenger!**
Ross rides south to meet Malcolm and Macduff, and he is thinking about the news he bears and the reception he is likely to get. He discusses with his companion, a lord, how he feels about having to deliver such an unwelcome message, and they try to decide on the best way to break the news to Macduff. In script form, write the conversation between Ross and the lord.

3 **'Tyrant, show thy face!'**
As Macduff, write an account of your thoughts and feelings as the battle outside Dunsinane Castle begins and you seek out Macbeth.

4 **What if ... ?**
History consists of events which might have turned out quite differently. For instance, in the story of Macbeth:
- what if Malcolm and Donalbain had stayed in Scotland?
- what if Banquo had spoken up about his suspicions?
- what if Macduff had not left for England?
- what if Edward the Confessor had not supported Malcolm?
- what if Macbeth had won the battle of Dunsinane?

Choose one of these suggestions, or one of your own if you prefer, and tell the story of what happened after this change of events.

Writing about the play: giving an opinion

Much of the writing you have done so far, in the ACTIVITIES sections of this book, and in English lessons in the past, has probably been personal (based on your own experiences), or descriptive (describing scenes and events). In some of the ACTIVITIES sections you are also asked to tackle a different kind of writing – writing in which you are asked to make a judgement about characters or events of the play.

Writing of this kind is roughly similar to a mathematical problem, but the good part about it is that there is no 'right' answer. Your opinion, if you can show your 'working out', is as good as anyone else's. The points that you make should 'add up' to your conclusion.

This is how a sum works:	This is how your writing works:
35+46+21+14	Introduction: what you are writing about
35	The first point you want to make
+	+
46	The second point you want to make
+	+
21	The third point you want to make
+	+
14	The fourth point you want to make
=	=
Answer	Conclusion: your 'answer' to the question

The questions on the opposite page give you an opportunity to practise this type of lay-out.

See also WRITING ABOUT CHARACTER (page 234)

Example:	**Was Macduff selfish to leave his family?**
	(Possible notes for essay)
Introduction	In a sentence or two, say what happened: Macduff to England (why?); family killed in his absence.

Point 1:	Lady Macduff is angry and regards Macduff's actions as desertion (include a quotation).
Point 2:	Macduff is acting for the good of the country (include a quotation) and this shows bravery.
Point 3:	If his mission is unsuccessful he knows he will be unable to return home (include a quotation).
Point 4:	He has no reason to suspect that Macbeth will order slaughter (possibly include a quotation).
Conclusion:	Macduff loyal, thoughtless, **not** selfish.

Questions

1 **One man's ambition – a national tragedy?**
Do you think that it is only Macbeth's ambition which drives him on and causes turmoil in Scotland, or are there other factors involved? If so, what are these other factors, and what influence do they have on the events of the play? (You will need to think about the witches' prophecies, Lady Macbeth, the apparitions and, of course, Macbeth's ambition.)

2 **Is Banquo responsible for his own downfall?**
What happens to Banquo? How well does he know Macbeth? Is he suspicious about the death of Duncan? Because he is a witness to the prophecies, should he anticipate what Macbeth will do next? Should he have been extra careful?

3 **Appearance and reality: an important element of the play?**
It has been said that there are many instances in the play when things are not what they seem; appearances cannot be trusted. (You can probably think immediately of the prophecies, the apparitions, and '*Look like th' innocent flower...*') Give detailed examples of occasions when there is a difference between appearance and reality, and say how important you think they are to the plot of *Macbeth*.

4 **Is it possible to stage Macbeth successfully in school?**
What are the difficulties – casting/technical (apparitions, ghost, swordfights)? How can they be overcome? Can the language and dramatic content be conveyed convincingly?

Writing about character

Sometimes you will be asked to do a piece of writing which is based on one character. Just as in WRITING ABOUT THE PLAY: GIVING AN OPINION, page 232, there are three points to remember:

1 The introduction makes clear to the reader that you have understood the title and know what you are writing about.

2 The 'body' of your writing leads the reader from one point to the next.

3 The conclusion is an 'answer' to the title, arrived at by weighing up the points you have made in 2. In the case of character writing you will need full character notes to work from. Organize your notes according to the title of the work.

If you are given the title *Malcolm* or *What sort of man is Malcolm?*, you might follow this outline:	If the title is a question such as *Will Malcolm be a good king?*, you must decide on your answer before you begin to write, and work towards that answer. Let us assume that your answer is *Yes*.
1 Introduction: say who Malcolm is.	1 Introduction: Malcolm named successor when relatively young
2 His second most important characteristic	2 Characteristics unfitting for a king
3 His minor characteristics	3 Characteristics which would make him a good king
4 His most important characteristic	
5 Conclusion: what sort of man he is	4 Conclusion: an 'answer' to the question of the title

Questions

1 **Macbeth:** '*This dead butcher*'
Malcolm speaks very unflatteringly of Macbeth at the end of
the play. You might think that his description is also very
accurate. At different times Macbeth is thought of as a hero
and a coward; the saviour of Scotland and the man who has
caused his country unbelievable anguish. How do you think of
him? What sort of man do you judge him to be?

2 **Lady Macbeth:** '*My dearest partner of greatness*'
Lady Macbeth proves to be a '*fiend-like queen*' according to
Malcolm, but is that simply because of the way in which she
and Macbeth came to the throne? What sort of queen would
she have been if Macbeth had succeeded to the throne as
named heir after Duncan's natural death? Do you think she has
the characteristics which would make her a good queen in
those circumstances.

3 **Duncan:** '*Born out of his proper age*'
One critic has said of Duncan:
'Born out of his proper age into a century of intrigue and
violence and offering a mark to rebels, traitors and ambitious
aspirants to the throne. He is of too refined and peaceful a
nature to cope with those who would contend with him.'
We know that he is referred to as '*the gracious Duncan*' in Act 3
scene 1 line 66 and '*most sainted King*' (Act 4 scene 3 line 109);
and at the beginning of Act 1 scene 7 Macbeth says he is
highly-respected. But, on balance, would you agree with the
critic that Duncan lacks the personality to rule effectively?

4 **Macduff:** '*Of all men else I have avoided thee*'
In Act 5 scene 8 Macbeth says he wants to shed no more
Macduff blood, but he should have avoided Macduff for other
reasons! What personal qualities does Macduff have which fit
him to be Macbeth's nemesis, and the means of restoring order
to Scotland?

Short questions

Sometimes you may be asked to write a short response to a question or topic. The topics below call for short pieces of writing (two paragraphs at the most). In each case you will need to pay close attention to a particular part of the play.

1 **Act 1 scene 3**
Why does Banquo not say more to Macbeth after lines 120–126? Does he misjudge Macbeth? Does he believe that he will not act on the prophecies but just watch the future with interest? Is there any guide in the rest of the scene that Macbeth will not merely sit back and watch?

2 **Act 1 scene 6**
Point out the examples of irony (or is it dramatic irony?) which run through this short scene.

3 **Act 2 scene 2**
Is there anything about Lady Macbeth's speech or manner in lines 1–13 which suggests that she is as uneasy as her husband concerning what is about to happen?

4 **Act 2 scene 3**
Give details about all the elements of disorder which are evident in this scene.

5 **Act 3 scene 3**
The assassins are referred to as 'murderers' in the previous scene, but is there any evidence here that they are, in fact, inexperienced at this sort of thing?

6 **Act 4 scene 1**
Explain how the whole scene is one of natural disorder: normality seems to be turned on its head (Macbeth's attitude to the witches, for instance). Can you give a reason for Macbeth's decision to order the killing of Macduff's family, which is surely the lowest of his low acts? Is it, perhaps, because of the atmosphere created earlier in the scene?

7 **Act 5 scene 6**
Malcolm tells Siward and his son to lead the army into battle. What are the various possible reasons for this

decision? Which reason do you feel is most likely to be the genuine one?

8 **Act 5 scene 8**

We have known from the beginning of the play that Macbeth has great prowess as a fighter, but Macduff's fighting qualities do not rate a mention. How is it that Macduff is able to kill Macbeth after a lengthy and tiring sword-fight?

9 **The whole play**

The witches need not have been on stage at all: their words could have been spoken by disembodied voices; or they could have been totally imaginary, speaking through other characters (as is the voice heard by Macbeth after killing Duncan). Why, then, does Shakespeare include the witches as characters? Do you think they are important enough to the plot to justify this? Is their physical presence on stage really necessary?

10 **The whole play**

When writing about another of Shakespeare's plays, *Julius Caesar*, a critic wrote of one character:

'He has all the characteristics of a tragic hero. A noble character stoops to conspiracy and, by errors of judgement, the product of his unpractical idealism, brings on himself and others defeat and death.'

Is Macbeth a 'hero'? Is he 'noble'? Re-write the paragraph, this time with Macbeth as the subject, changing as few words as possible.

Glossary

Alarum: A call to arms, often a trumpet call.

Alliteration: A figure of speech in which a number of words close to each other in a piece of writing begin with the same sound:

'*Will I with wine and wassail so convince*'

Alliteration helps to draw attention to these words.

Anachronism: In a historical drama the writer may accidentally or deliberately allow characters to refer to things from a later period, which they would not have known about. This is called 'anachronism':

'*Till he disbursed, at Saint Colme's Inch,*
Ten thousand dollars to our general use.'

Dollars were sixteenth-century coins, not eleventh-century.

Antithesis: A figure of speech in which the writer brings two opposite or contrasting ideas up against each other:

'*Nothing in his life*
Became him like the leaving it; he died
As one that had been studied in his death,
To throw away the dearest thing he owed,
As 'twere a careless trifle.'

Apostrophe: When a character suddenly speaks directly to someone or something, which may or may not be present:

'*Stars hide your fires*'

Blank verse: See page 224

Dramatic irony: A situation in a play when the audience (and possibly some of the characters) know something that one or more of the characters don't. In a pantomime, for example, young children will often shout to tell the heroine that a dreadful monster is creeping up behind her, unseen.

An example from *Macbeth* is when Duncan arrives at Macbeth's castle and says what a healthy place it is. We know that Macbeth and Lady Macbeth intend that it should be most unhealthy for Duncan.

Exeunt: A Latin word meaning 'They go away', used for the departure of characters from a scene.

Exit: A Latin word meaning 'S/he goes away', used for the departure of a character from a scene.

Hyperbole: Deliberate exaggeration, for dramatic effect.

> *'The multiplying villainies of nature*
> *Do swarm upon him'*

Irony: When someone says one thing and means another, often to make fun of, tease, or satirize someone else:

> *'Who cannot want the thought, how monstrous*
> *It was for Malcolm and for Donalbain*
> *To kill their gracious father? Damned fact.*
> *How it did grieve Macbeth!'*

See also DRAMATIC IRONY

Metaphor: A figure of speech in which one person, or thing, or idea is described as if it were another.

> *'The Thane of Cawdor lives. Why do you dress me*
> *In borrowed robes?'*

Macbeth is saying that the title of Thane of Cawdor does not belong to him, any more than someone else's clothes would.

Onomatopoeia: Using words that are chosen because they mimic the sound of what is being described:

> *'Double, double toil and trouble;*
> *Fire burn, and cauldron bubble.'*

The sound of the boiling cauldron runs through these two lines.

Oxymoron: A figure of speech in which the writer combines two ideas which are opposites. This frequently has a startling or unusual effect:

> *'Fair is foul, and foul is fair'*

Personification: Referring to a thing or an idea as if it were a person:

> *'Time, thou anticipat'st my dread exploits.'*

Play on words: see PUN

Pun: A figure of speech in which the writer uses a word that has more than one meaning. Both meanings of the word are used to make a joke. In Act 2 scene 3, the porter pretends that he is keeper of Hell Gate and he welcomes a tailor with the words, '*Here you may roast your goose*'. A 'goose' is a tailor's iron, so the porter is telling him that he has come to the right place to warm it; and when someone's 'goose is cooked', it means that all is lost. Sometimes a pun may be used to make a more serious point. Lady Macbeth takes the daggers back to Duncan's chamber, saying that she will smear the guards' faces with blood (gold was thought of as red):

> '*If he do bleed,*
> *I'll gild the faces of the grooms withal,*
> *For it must seem their guilt.*'

Simile: A comparison between two things which the writer makes clear by using words such as 'like' or 'as':

> '*Doubtful it stood,*
> *As two spent swimmers, that do cling together*
> *And choke their art.*'

Soliloquy: When a character is alone on stage, or separated from the other characters in some way and speaks apparently to himself or herself.